"Discerning and deeply humane, these essays from international award-winning poet, activist, author Margaret Randall are gems of wisdom, originality, and vision, challenging us to rethink the very process of thought itself. Distilled with age and her wide-ranging art and activism over the course of eight decades, these pieces are quintessential Randall: profound, moving, unforgettable."

— Minrose Gwin, author of *The Accidentals*

"In *Thinking about Thinking*, Margaret Randall's brilliant mind takes us on a journey of exploration of the personal: identity, vulnerability, purpose; and of the social/political (which of course is personal): revolution, food, art, technology. From the personal 'Becoming Elizabeth Taylor' to the provocative 'Preserving Racism or Preserving History?' to the expansive, research-based 'Breaking the Maya Code: Creativity across Continents and Time,' to the exquisite love letter to her wife Barbara, 'Silliness Gene,' the thirty-one essays will school you, challenge you, tickle you, entertain you, and give you hope. Grateful to take this journey with someone so deeply committed to speaking her truth, in the service of setting herself, and others, free."

— Olga Talamante, community activist and Executive Director Emerita of the Chicana Latina Foundation

"Margaret Randall's *Thinking about Thinking* takes us into the mind of one of the most courageous and nuanced political and cultural thinkers of our era. That she is also one of the world's greatest living poets gives the language of these exquisite essays a precision and grace not found in most philosophic writing. Those of us discouraged by modern philosophy's linguistic and logical reductionism will find Randall's essays to be inspiring thought-expeditions into realms of conscience, contradiction, and meaning. They stimulate us to explore the roots of our own thought processes, take notice of the exceptions we have to our own positions, and think with greater confidence and deeper curiosity about our own ways of making sense of the world. Randall's 'mind wanderings,' as she calls them, are directed at finding the truth and how she feels about it, the truth with all its subtle self-contradictions, its delicate shadings, and the emphatic resonance we feel when it finally reveals itself in a form we can comprehend. In *Thinking about Thinking*, Margaret Randall leads by example; she shows us with clarity and an anti-dogmatic openness-of-mind new ways to deal with the full spectrum of our reactions to the way life presents itself to our consciousness and ways of ordering our thoughts. Rarely is a book both beautiful and practical. Randall's is just that—a moving and revelatory exploration of some of the world's great conundrums, and a trail guide to how any one of us might move through the underbrush and into open spaces and new light."

– V. B. Price, author of *Innocence Regained*
and columnist at mercmessenger.com

Thinking

about Thinking

Selected books by Margaret Randall

Essays

Haydée Santamaría, Cuban Revolutionary: She Lived by Transgression

Che on My Mind

To Change the World: My Years in Cuba

The Price You Pay: The Hidden Cost of Women's Relationship to Money

Gathering Rage: The Failure of Twentieth Century Revolutions to Develop a Feminist Agenda

The Shape of Red *(with Ruth Hubbard)*

Poetry

Out of Violence into Poetry

Starfish on a Beach: The Pandemic Poems

Time's Language: Selected Poems, 1959-2018

About Little Charlie Lindbergh and Other Poems

As If the Empty Chair/Como si la silla vacía

This Is about Incest

Oral History

When I Look into the Mirror and See You: Women, Terror & Resistance

Sandino's Daughters Revisited

Christians in the Nicaraguan Revolution

Sandino's Daughters

Spirit of the People: Vietnamese Women Two Years from the Geneva Accords

Thinking **Margaret Randall** about Thinking

not quite essays

Casa Urraca Press
A B I Q U I U

Copyright © 2021 by Margaret Randall

All rights reserved.

Thank you for supporting authors and artists by buying an authorized edition of this book and respecting all copyright laws by not reproducing, scanning, or distributing any part of it in any form without permission from the author or artist directly or via the publisher, except as permitted by fair use. You are empowering artists to keep creating, and Casa Urraca Press to keep publishing, books for readers like you who actually look at copyright pages.

Cover photograph by Magdalena Lily McCarson.
Set in Nobel and Marion.

First edition, v. 1.1

ISBN 978-1-7351516-4-9
Ebook ISBN 978-1-7351516-5-6

CASA URRACA PRESS

an imprint of Casa Urraca, Ltd.
PO Box 1119
Abiquiu, New Mexico 87510
casaurracaltd.com

This book is for
Guillermo Manuel Martín Álvarez Randall
and Emma Nahuí Álvarez Randall,
my great-grandchildren, who are too young to read it now
but are already thinking creatively about thinking.

Contents

About these texts	*xiii*
Never Quite	5
The Horse and the Eighteen-Wheeler	11
Preserving Racism or Preserving History?	19
Our Time Has Come... with a Few Caveats	31
Homunculus	41
Becoming Elizabeth Taylor	45
Where Was That Again?	49
Mapping Our Lives	55
Six Degrees of Separation	61
Calling Paulo Freire	69
Land	77
Disaster's False Dichotomy	81
Our Little Secret	89
I Told You It Wouldn't End Well	95
Naming Ourselves	101
Makeover	109
The Age of Lies	115

Was Shakespeare a Political Poet?	*123*
The Dictator	*131*
Alan Turing, or, the Fear of Difference	*137*
Breaking the Maya Code:	
Creativity across Continents and Time	*143*
How We Feed Ourselves	*153*
Eating Out	*163*
Farewell to the Book?	*169*
What Were They Thinking?	*175*
Silliness Gene	*183*
What Would They Say?	*187*
Starfish on the Beach: A Fable for 2020	*193*
On the Gender Spectrum	*195*
Art and Technology through Time and Space	*203*
Abandoning Either/Or	*231*
Acknowledgments	*239*
About the author	*241*

About these texts

ESSAYS? NOT QUITE. Fully researched and documented academic treatises? No. Perhaps musings? More deliberate and developed. Some composite that challenges the more conventional literary genres? I hope so.

These texts, most of them shorter than the usual essay, range over a variety of subjects. Almost all are spinoffs from a word or idea, something that appeared in a dream, struck me while conversing about an entirely unrelated issue or when engulfed in the silence in which I immerse myself while exercising or just before giving myself to sleep. Some are urgent responses to the problems we live with today.

I don't meditate. I've tried the practice and acknowledge its benefits for many, but have never been able to sufficiently empty my mind. There's always that bit of cadmium red teasing at the far corner of my vision or a sudden movement that takes me somewhere on the wings of memory. Most meditative practices are also religious in nature, and I tend to shy away from anything that smacks of religion. My mind wanderings are more personal and also more practical.

"Never Quite" and "Homunculus" were the first pieces I wrote for this collection. Others quickly followed. Some, like "Our Time Has Come," "Abandoning Either/Or," "On the Gender Spectrum," "Preserving Racism or Preserving History?" and "Was Shakespeare a Political Poet?" are relatively current. "Art and Technology through Time and Space" is the most recent. Some respond to current events, immediate and dramatic as the wars we resist, the prospect of losing our habitat, or the COVID-19 pandemic that assaulted us just as I was gathering these texts into book form. As the crisis unfolded, its sudden and overwhelming nature kept provoking my need to respond. Other pieces address issues I have grappled with most of my adult life and some when I was still a child. They reflect my passions and what I want to be saying about them as I move through my ninth decade. In this era of flagrant lies and so-called fake news, I believe it is more than ever important to make sure that every word we utter means exactly what we intend it to say.

— Albuquerque, December 2020

Speak—
But do not split the No from the Yes.
Give your saying also meaning:
Give it its shadow.[1]

– Paul Celan

It matters what stories we tell to tell other stories with;
it matters what concepts we think
to think other concepts with.[2]

– Donna Haraway

---

1. "Speak, You Too." *Memory Rose into Threshold Speech*, trans. Pierre Joris. Farrar, Straus and Giroux, 2020, p. 149.

2. *Staying with the Trouble*. Duke University Press, 2016, p 118.

Never Quite

I AM REACHING BACK THROUGH TIME AND SPACE, my outstretched arms flailing through a murky sea, heaving and tossing. Objects, broken or whole, collide with me, although there is no danger of damage inflicted. This is not a physical exercise but one of the senses, the mind. Time seems to expand and contract, but no discrete event comes into focus. I am searching for something elusive—whether I give it my utmost concentration or the freedom of totally letting go.

Some would surely search for their birth, that volatile frontier between amniotic waters and first gulp of air. Or a preview of their death. These are frontiers about which humans have wondered since the beginning of time. There are plenty of tales, none of which have ever seemed reliable to me: too unimaginative, too clichéd, too much in the mold of religious dogma. Besides, I am sure memory itself works differently on either side of those impenetrable lines, its function and exercise operating by rules we cannot know.

Too much to expect our memories to bridge such disparate territories.

I am also less ambitious. Seeking out less dramatic, more conscious, change. For example, it would be a welcome accomplishment were I simply able to distinguish those words that first gave name to colors and how I responded to them. Mother would have pointed to ordinary objects, encouraging me with a question such as "What color is this?" and after much trial and error I would have responded in a way that fit the question, causing her a smile of pride and satisfaction as my infant voice announced "blue" or "red." What was my perception like before I was able to give these answers?

First color or number. First ability to link two or three words in something that could be called a sentence. First identification of words on a page. First successful effort to produce those words myself. First utterance completely of my own creation. First narrative. First successful lie. Such moments as these are the ones I would retrieve now, through the long fog of eighty-four years of mindless accumulation. The muddled moment before, and illuminated one after, learning to read. The before and after that outlined in brilliant light an understanding of how I might add a dart of my own discovery to someone else's equation. Learning to sit up or crawl or walk: such physical advances seem rote by comparison. It's the imaginative moment of just-attained consciousness I hope to lay bare, repossess.

The impossible journey began this morning as I lay on the couch, eyes half closed, trying to heal from a flu that beat me to submission more than a week ago. Fever can free one's thought process, level the playing field, and remove obstacles standing in the way. It was February of 2020, and I had recently returned on a very long flight from Uruguay.

In retrospect, I may have come down with a mild form of the coronavirus, not yet in most of the world's vocabulary. COVID-19 or not, at times I was near delirium.

My mind traveled to the unknown and unrecorded instant when for the first time I didn't simply understand that one train of thought or another was logical, believable, important, but injected something of my own into the exploration, thus expanding or changing the direction of its meaning. A creation of my own, building upon knowledge itself, that ragged tangle: millennia of linked ideas, a patchwork beginning long before written history and continuing seamlessly into a future that may or may not come to be. That moment in which I may claim my place in the storyline. Impossibly elusive and at once deeply precious.

The nature of human aging seems to erase initial memories even as it acquires new ones. We lose those made early on as we replace them with those of more recent vintage. A reversal of sorts occurs in people diagnosed with dementia: they may lose more recent recollections while retaining or revisiting those made long ago, often surprising loved ones resigned only to loss. So little is known about such painful memory change, and it is so often misinterpreted, that generalizing about the phenomenon leads us into dead-end conjecture at best.

As I ponder this, I realize that what most interests me are not really those break-out moments in which I was first able to identify a color or decipher a word on the page. For years, throughout early and middling adulthood, I walked an increasingly complex map on which I waded through choices: does this or that explanation for the mystery of life seem more reasonable? Who among the thinkers who have gone before inspires the most confidence in me? Who can I follow? Whose thinking must I shed? At some point, following was not enough. I needed to lead, or at least to be part of the leading contingent. And I found myself adding a question here, an idea there. I recognized my own ability to shape the conversation.

A lot of it is about passion. And questions, our reluctance or readiness to ask them. We are conditioned to believe our world is peopled by experts who have all the answers and the rest of us who are destined to follow their advice. And so, we have situations such as that of the famous British anthropologist Eric Thompson who, in the nineteenth century, set the work on the decipherment of Maya glyphs back at least one hundred years because no one dared challenge the direction of his research—which turned out to be wrong. Or the respected linguist Noam Chomsky, a century later, who posited that language acquisition was in our DNA. That, too, turned out to be an erroneous assumption, delaying research in the field by decades. Our great thinkers deserve our admiration. But anyone can be fallible with regard to one or more aspects of a problem, and discovery often comes from unexpected sources. Questioning is a vital part of learning. In an educational system designed to produce mimics rather than original thinkers, it is rarely encouraged.

I have come to understand that today's extreme specialization fragments the connective tissue that renders the map readable. Contrary to common assumption, the more we concentrate on each piece of the whole, the less we may understand. The more holistic our approach, the easier it is to enter underpasses, detours, and byways, cross bridges, and wander footpaths. A sure-footed mountain goat may lead us along the faintest of trails. A mole may take us beneath the earth's surface into its hidden abode where there is no light, only sensation. If we could bring ourselves to be humbler, if we respected the smallest ideas and were willing to move as easily into them as into the largest, we might be surprised at what we find. If we could resist reductionist thinking for holistic vision, we might be able to go further.

And so I search, allowing my mind to wander through my years, ignoring limitations born of class, culture, race, gender, and habit. No direction is left unimagined, no pathway is too insignificant. I may yet find a sliver of what I seek. If I do, I hope I don't let it slip through my fingers out of ignorance, intimidation, failure of the imagination, lack of confidence, or fear.

Sometimes we can only really see with our eyes closed.

The Horse and the
Eighteen-Wheeler

THE WRITER EDWARD ABBEY was best known for masterpieces such as *Desert Solitaire* and *The Monkey Wrench Gang*. But we went to the University of New Mexico together in the 1950s and I remember an earlier novel, now forgotten by all but a few devoted fans. *The Brave Cowboy*, published in 1956, is a Western story at the end of which the protagonist gallops out of the Sandia Mountains east of Albuquerque headed for Mexico. Just as he crosses Tijeras Canyon, braving the traffic on what was once old Route 66, he is hit by an eighteen-wheeler barreling through. After Abbey became famous, *The Brave Cowboy* was made into a movie with Kirk Douglas playing the lead.

Those who believe in fate assume that the journeys of horseman and truck were predestined to collide at that moment and in that place. Those, like myself, who favor chance would say the two just happened to be in the wrong place at the wrong time. The collision was a terrible accident. Either way, its impact on rider, horse, and truck driver would have been the same. But its implications for the way we think about the sudden turns our lives may take couldn't be more different.

Some people claim that everything happens for a reason. This belief extends even to such horrific episodes as the Nazi Holocaust and the Cambodian Genocide. For atrocities such as these, unabashed power abuse, extreme racism or classism, and a particular sort of political moment must converge.

Those who credit fate generally believe in God. When asked to explain how an all-loving deity can allow such things to take place, they respond with some version of: "He works in mysterious ways," "It isn't for us to question," or "We must have faith." Or perhaps they simply explain it more secularly by saying: "What's meant to be is meant to be."

Those of us who are inclined to interpret Abbey's story scientifically believe that an unforeseen, meaningful, shocking, or even fortuitous collision—of people, events, or ideas—is the result of an infinite number of variables that bring the principals together by chance. Something like the butterfly effect, by which small things can have non-linear impacts on a complex system.

Each occurrence depends on the one before. And each can no more be predicted than prevented—or provoked. They include everything from the Big Bang to the surge of love I feel for my wife and the kisses we exchange. The brave cowboy and the trucker are fictional, but such events happen every day in real life.

On August 14, 1997, twelve European hikers set out to explore the northern Arizona desert and its canyons. Most were from France, one each from England and Switzerland. A local man warned the group not to enter a narrow limestone slot, but their Los Angeles-based guide, Pancho Quintane, couldn't imagine why. He looked up at the sky, which was cloudless. Later, Benson Nez, a ranger on the Navajo reservation, confirmed that: "Rain hadn't fallen where they were hiking."

The storm came without warning. A cloudburst fifteen miles away sent heavy runoff down a normally dry stream bed in Antelope Canyon and toward the unsuspecting hikers. It caught them in a narrow slot canyon from which there was no escape; an eleven-foot wall of muddy water, slurry, and fast-moving debris killed most of them instantly. Only the guide escaped with his life. His clothes had been ripped from him. He was battered and bloody but alive. All the others perished. One woman's body was later found miles away in Lake Powell. Several of the bodies were never recovered.

People think of the desert as a dry place where loss of life is due to dehydration. That is true. But it is also a place where one can die by drowning. For the latter to happen, the elements must come together in a perfect recipe for death. Not fate but random occurrences.

I remember another moment of sudden rain, not tragic but illuminating. An eighteen-wheeler played its part in this one as well. In 1963, the great National Museum of Anthropology was being built in Mexico City's Chapultepec Park. It was decided that the immense statue of the rain god Tlaloc, found a century earlier in a dry stream bed near the town of Coatlinchán in the state of Mexico, should be placed at the museum's entrance. And so, on April 16, 1964, the statue, weighing 168 tons and standing twenty-three feet tall when upright, was mounted on a specially conditioned truck bed and began its journey to the capital.

I was one of the twenty-five thousand onlookers lining the streets the day Tlaloc arrived. The sky was a brilliant blue. It was the dry season and there wasn't a sign of rain. As the statue made its slow way through the city's central plaza—the Zócalo, where the Aztec pyramid of Tenochtitlán once stood—torrents of water suddenly descended from that clear blue. This was, after all, the rain god. I don't think anyone there that day thought the downpour strange. Many may have believed it to be a supernatural event. I believe it to have responded to some law of nature we do not yet understand because we are so unwilling to consider any but our Western scientific approach.

Even those of us who believe in chance understand that there are forces and motives that lead to fortuitous or ominous collisions. I am thinking now of yet another eighteen-wheeler, this one thundering along an almost empty stretch of road that runs south to north through New Mexico Navajo country near the Arizona border. One night some years back, a young man named Aaron, desperate about life prospects he must have felt powerless to control, got drunk and ran out into the pathway of that truck. The driver, horrified, slammed on his brakes but was unable to stop in time. Aaron's suicide, like those of far too many Native American youths, was preordained in a way. Not by fate, but by a neocolonialist system that punishes the poor in a profoundly racist society. You can only imagine that this sort of tragedy is about destiny if you believe the few deserve everything while the many remain bereft of opportunity. Or that poverty exists because some people are lazy or don't work hard enough.

I am fascinated by the disparate journeys that bring people, locations, events, or ideas together at a particular moment. I have gone to places where history was being made and ended up living in those places during periods of dramatic social change. Such experiences allowed me to understand the world in ways I wouldn't have otherwise. When people asked me how or why I took that route, I used to say: "I guess I just happened to be in the right place at the right time." I don't say that anymore. I have come to understand it wasn't true.

I didn't just happen to land among the abstract expressionist artists and poets who were inventing a new creative language in the New York City of the late 1950s or to travel the length of North Vietnam during the last six months of the U.S. American war there. I didn't just happen to go to Cuba during that country's second decade of revolution, or to Nicaragua during its first years of Sandinista struggle. I chose to be in those vibrant places at those historic moments. Not fate or destiny, but idealism, curiosity, and decision determined my choices.

In the same way, every major event in my life has been based on choice, a conscious determination to nurture or create. I chose to have each of my children. I resolved to be a writer. I decided to join the struggle for justice wherever I was and whether or not my decision was what today we would call politically correct or would lead to "success" in the traditional sense of that word. Perhaps—more unusual for the time—I made up my mind, even as a woman, that I didn't have to choose between motherhood and becoming a writer, or between being interested in the world from a position of armchair comfort and trying to change it. I could and would do it all.

I never thought twice about embracing feminism or assuming my lesbian identity. When, upon my return to the United States after almost a quarter century in Latin America, the U.S. government ordered me deported because of opinions expressed in some of my books, I didn't hesitate to stay and fight or do whatever I had to in order to win. I have never shied away from difficult choices when I felt they were the right ones for me.

I am not claiming some sort of prophetic vision. In retrospect, some of my decisions may have turned out to be errors or awkward detours. But making them, often spontaneously, has mostly made me proud and imbued my life with a momentum that gives me the courage to continue.

Just as there are instances of people coming together in ways that change everything, there are also instances of the opposite: meetings that should have happened but didn't, connections that failed. I had a close friend who, during World War II, sent her young son to the French countryside to save him from Germany's fascist takeover of Paris. After the war, they were supposed to be reunited at a specific railway station, but that reunion never happened. She waited on the platform in vain. He didn't get off the train. Was he on that train and somehow missed the stop, or on another? Was she at the wrong station or the right station but the wrong platform? Many years passed. The mother learned to live without her son, the son without his mother. But the son never forgave the missed meeting he believed had been her fault. Both lives were forever changed.

When things, usually bad things, happen, we sometimes say it was "a perfect storm." We mean a series of events—a missed signal or train, a misunderstood word or phrase, something occurring moments too soon or too late, sudden weather, direction of wind or water, a narrow slot canyon or crowded beach, a big wave—combined to produce the conditions required for a particular outcome. Lacking any one of those conditions, the outcome would have been different.

But there are other sorts of perfect storms, as well, those that bring people together even when the likelihood of a connection is remote. I often wonder about the chance circumstances in which my relationship with the woman I've loved for thirty-four years began. We couldn't have been more different in terms of age, class, and culture. From an upper middle-class family, I was a traveler recently returned home and in the midst of a demanding legal battle. Barbara worked in a sign shop but liked taking a university course each semester to keep herself intellectually stimulated. In 1985, she went to the University of New Mexico's Women's

Studies Program and asked the secretary to recommend a class.

The secretary recommended Women and Creativity, a course I was teaching. Barbara enrolled. I was intrigued by her purple overalls and yellow sneakers as well as her insightful contributions to class discussion. After final grades had been turned in, she came to my office with a single rose hidden in her gym bag. I was moved. I asked her to dinner. She accepted. The rest is history. If she or I had reacted differently, the story wouldn't have ended as it did.

When elements or people unite in this way, it behooves us to consider the variables: velocity, temperature, intention, chemistry, and so forth. We're talking science or coincidence here, not fate. When people, places, or ideas collide, there is always a reason or series of reasons that leads to the collision. Reason, not some higher power. Our will, not that exercised by a fictitious god, determines who we are and what we do with our brief passage through this life.

Preserving Racism or Preserving History?

IN THE 1940s AND '50s, when I was growing up in Albuquerque, New Mexico, monuments to the Pioneer Mother graced public parks in many western cities. They had a traditional aesthetic; the mother with her bonnet and long skirt swirling about her ankles seemed to be in the midst of taking a determined stride. She often carried an infant in her arms and had two or more young children at her feet. Most of the sculptors who produced these statues were mediocre at best. I have yet to see one that can be considered great art. Still, I remember being moved by Albuquerque's Madonna of the Trail, as she was called. As a young middle-class white girl just coming into womanhood in the stifling 1950s, I often stopped to gaze at her in one of the city's downtown parks.

The monument bore an inscription plate that spoke of the courage and fortitude of those women who "opened up the west." Nowhere did it mention the westward thrust's encroachment on and abuse of Native Americans, nor the crimes committed in the name of colonization. I discovered the sordid side of this history as I grew older and, as a young adult, began to be able to situate my country's westward exploration within an expansionist and racist framework. But the pioneer woman retained her courage in my heart. I knew she had faced untold hardships. And I already intuited that women in the westward push, just like women in all situations throughout history, suffered misogynist culture and gender inequities. I also knew that the pioneer woman's story was but a single strand of those that make up the fabric of my country's past.

Looking back, I understand that I can only explain the pioneer woman's impact on me by referencing my emotional response. Years before, as a very small female child, I had gazed up at the imposing stone figure of the Winged Victory of Samothrace on loan to a New York City museum and placed atop its broad staircase. The statue's glorious wings and forward thrust of body spoke to me of my own incipient longings, the life I would be able to create if I could access my inner power. The pioneer woman evoked in me this same sense of possibility, empowerment in a world in which my gender was treated as a liability.

In spring 2020, following a very long list of crimes in which mostly Black men and women were summarily murdered by mostly white police, an anti-racist protest movement exploded across the United States. Led by Black Lives Matter, thousands poured into the streets and stayed there far longer than previous movements. The protestors were tired of promises. They demanded change. They wanted city and state governments to defund out-of-control police departments, and they advocated for community oversight of law and order. In more general terms, they were rebelling against a neofascist and profoundly racist government.

These protests also focused on statues that for decades—in some cases centuries—paid tribute to racist figures in our history. Demands for removal of these statues made me think back to my infatuation with Albuquerque's Pioneer Mother, and forward to a time when our monuments may truly reflect who we want to be as a nation.

Most statues of Jefferson Davis, the president of our short-lived Confederacy, or Robert E. Lee, the general who led the southern troops to defeat in our Civil War, were erected in the immediate aftermath of that conflict, when those who funded and built them wanted to remind the public that, despite the loss of the Confederacy, the idea of owning slaves was still deeply embedded in their cultural consciousness. Others were erected later in the nineteenth century by the United Daughters of the Confederacy.[1] Whatever their origin, the statues were meant to intimidate. Emancipation was the law of the land on paper, but discrimination in all its forms would be with us for generations, and those monuments wouldn't let the descendants of slaves forget it. A century and a half after humans kidnapped in Africa and brought to the U.S. as slave labor were freed, Black Americans continue to suffer many sorts of segregation, an unequal level of poverty, police brutality, inferior educations, the lowest paid jobs, and the least accessible health care. Black males today are 34% of our prison population, but Black men and women are only 13.4% of the general population.

Statues to the heroes of the Confederacy are symbolic of this racist reality. Every Black person who has to pass one on their way to work each day is reminded that white America, by and large, continues to consider them second-class citizens. The same is true for the military members

---

1. The United Daughters of the Confederacy is an American hereditary association of Southern women established in Nashville, Tennessee, in 1894. It has been labeled neo-Confederate by the Southern Poverty Law Center, which monitors hate groups and extremists.

who train or work on bases bearing the names of racist heroes; it is a constant reminder that they are expected to be willing to die for their country while being forced to honor the historic figures who believed them inferior.

Does white America solve its race problem by changing names and removing statues? It's a start, but we need much more than that. We need education, and we need to stop othering stigmatized groups, thus preventing them from voicing their experience on a par with everyone else. We need education that includes real history and critical thinking, a frank national conversation about race, and a government dedicated to finding solutions rather than perpetuating stereotypes and punishing minorities. But is it not also dangerous for us to erase the embarrassing or criminal chapters in our history, to pretend they never happened, and to continue to avoid discussing them in any useful way? Right-wingers call the removal of statues part of "cancel culture"; it is their way of disguising their racist intentions, arguing that they have only the preservation of history at heart so the statues and brand labels and team names and other remnants of racist culture should endure. This is an absurd definition, but I don't believe blanket removal is the answer.

Some of the figures whose names adorn public monuments are difficult to regard as all good or all bad. Christopher Columbus, for example, was a great explorer as well as the man we credit with imposing a colonialist culture on the original peoples of this land. Other countries, too, have similar problems. Lenin developed a sociopolitical and economic system that is arguably fairer to the vast majority of people. But revolution also attempted to do away with class stratification and meant death for many. The collapse of the Soviet Union in 1989–1990 brought with it the immediate demolition of busts and statues of Lenin.

Now, after years of corrupt capitalism, some of these are being returned to their pedestals.

There are examples, of course, of figures who were so evil that there is no question that removing all public tribute to them is socially healthy. Hitler would be one, Pol Pot another. In New Mexico, where I live, there were several large statues of Juan de Oñate, a sixteenth-century conquistador who marched into the territory plundering and murdering the natives on behalf of Crown and Cross. In 1598, Oñate cut the right feet off of young men at Acoma Pueblo and sent several dozen young women to Mexico City as slaves. At the height of the 2020 protests, these Oñate statues were finally torn down, and the University of New Mexico removed Oñate's name from one of its buildings. Some racist members of the conservative Hispanic community are angry about these changes. For anyone conscious of the crimes committed against Native Americans in this part of the country, the removals didn't come soon enough. The thirty-six-foot-tall statue of Oñate in El Paso, Texas, has been called the largest equestrian statue in the world. In the face of protests over the years, and in an effort to placate its critics, its name was changed to "The Equestrian." It has not yet been taken down, but protestors in June of 2020 did deface it with red paint, which has since been removed.

In California, we had statues honoring Junipero Serra (1713–1784), a Franciscan and the principal architect of the California mission system during the era of Spanish colonization. Serra used forced Native labor, beat and otherwise mistreated indigenous converts, and presided over a brutal colonialist subjugation from San Diego north. Nevertheless, Pope John Paul II beatified Serra in 1988 and Pope Francis canonized him in 2015. Statues of the saint proliferated. At the height of the 2020 protests, about five dozen indigenous activists of all ages gathered at Father

Serra Park in downtown Los Angeles. A Tataviam/Chumash elder named Alan Salazar burned sage and invoked the spirits of his ancestors. A group of young activists bound the statue of Serra with ropes and tore him from his base. Then they placed sage and other offerings where the statue had been and turned its empty pedestal into an altar to equality and hope for the future.

From 1966 to 1976, Chinese leader Mao Zedong launched what he called the Cultural Revolution, a period during which, in the name of doing away with bourgeois values, hundreds of thousands of intellectuals, artists, and others who revered a cultural past lost their jobs and were sent to reeducation camps, forced into slave labor, imprisoned, or killed. Children were urged to report on their parents. Even many Communist Party members suffered. Today in China there are at least two museums I know of that tell a history of the period. The museum in Shantou honors the many who lost their lives during the Cultural Revolution. The current iteration of the Chinese Communist Party would seem to approve of the place. The sign at the entrance to this museum reads: "The Cultural Revolution Was a Mistake." Near the city of Chengdu, the Jianchuan Museum Cluster marks the same period, but it carries a narrower and more ambiguous reading of that siege of terror. On the four pillars that support the museum gate it says: "Remember war for peace. Remember lessons for the future. Remember disasters for serenity. Remember folk customs for heritage." This motto would seem to imply that the horrors of the Cultural Revolution were necessary to bring about a serene and peaceful present.

There is no question in my mind that all aspects of our history must be preserved. The many monuments and museums dedicated to the mid-twentieth-century Jewish Holocaust have certainly not prevented subsequent genocides, but they preserve a memory that is essential to our humanity. Auschwitz and other Nazi concentration camps became sites of remembrance shortly after the end of the war. Cambodia's Killing Fields are memorialized in all their horror; the very site where the atrocities were perpetrated has been turned into a place of reverence. It has gardens and pagodas but also a temple filled with hundreds of skulls. When it rains, the earth bleeds bits of clothing, teeth, and fragments of bone of the million and a half who were assassinated there. The memory of Latin America's Dirty Wars of the 1970s and '80s are preserved in moving monuments to the tens of thousands of Disappeared. Museums of Memory in Argentina, Uruguay, Chile, and other Latin American countries display relics and photographs—and truth. For the survivors in all these places whose lives were forever altered by these atrocities, such memorials are necessary.

As our political scene changes, the popular sense of what these monuments, statues, team names, brands, and memorials mean may also change in the popular consciousness. Interpretation is rooted in the political culture in power at any given time. It is visceral, imprinted on the DNA of those affected. Important questions are: If today's protestors are rising up against discrimination and injustice—in the present as well as in the past—are there ever instances in which the removal of a statue or monument goes too far, taking with it pieces of history that must be left in view in order to be understood? Should an understanding of right and wrong change as the political winds blow? Cannot human beings agree that colonialism, slavery, extermination camps, torture, and mass murder are always wrong?

Of course, monuments and memorials correspond to who is telling the story. I think of the Vietnam Veterans Memorial in Washington, D.C. Maya Lin designed a powerful v-shaped black granite structure that emerges from the earth at either end as it rises to a high point at its apex. On this wall, as it is frequently called, are inscribed the names of the fifty-eight thousand U.S. military personnel who died in Vietnam during that protracted and ultimately unpopular war. Relatives and friends come to contemplate their losses. Many make rubbings of the names of loved ones on small squares of paper available for that purpose. People also leave offerings: everything from trinkets of one kind or another to flowers and poems. Visiting this monument is a participatory experience, and one might call it a successful memorial.

But what of the Vietnamese who died in that long conflagration? Whole villages were firebombed by an invading army. Children were napalmed. Large areas of land were rendered barren for decades; nothing grew. No matter how meaningful the Vietnam Veterans Memorial is to U.S. citizens affected by that war, I would argue that all lives lost were precious. But I doubt if Maya Lin would have received the commission had she designed a monument honoring the Vietnamese as well as American dead.

And this really gets to the core of the issue: U.S. soldiers in Vietnam were heroes to some but criminals to others. Or, if not criminals, then cannon fodder in the service of criminals conducting imperialist or genocidal wars. The Vietnamese patriots were considered our enemy by some but were defending their nation from invasion. It's the dual significance of the monuments that creates the problem. If we simply accept them as good or bad, depending on our point of view, we are echoing an "us and them" discourse that keeps us from understanding history. This is why, whether we tear down the statues or remove them to a place where an analysis of their historic significance can be added to their display, we need an in-depth discussion that includes information about when they were erected, by whom, and for what purpose. It is the powerful of any era who create these monuments. And when the people attack them, they are rebelling against those who erected the statues and against those who continue their policies. The protestors are rising up against criminal power, which is a good thing. It is important that they don't also, unwittingly or not, rise up against history.

Thinking about our Vietnam monument, I wondered if a war anywhere has been memorialized by honoring those lost on both sides. I found that there are two such monuments in the state of Kentucky: the Veteran's Monument in Covington, erected in 1933, and the Confederate-Union Veterans' Memorial at the Butler County Courthouse in Morgantown, erected in 1907. These sites honor the fallen from both armies in our Civil War. Perhaps this was made possible by the fact that the Confederacy and the Union reunited as a single nation. In our fragmented and xenophobic world, it may be too much to ask that we pay tribute to the dead of two different countries in a single memorial.

For generations, Custer's Last Stand and the sites of other battles between the U.S. Army and Native Americans told only the white man's story. In recent times, Native tribes have added their versions of history or placed alternative memorials nearby. They have also been successful at getting a number of major museums to return sacred tribal artifacts and human remains. Despite these attempts at memory retrieval and rectification, the white man's version of history remains predominant. It is almost always the one told in the history books, at site museums, and on monuments.

There are many other ways in which stories remain incomplete in memorials to a particular historic event. President John F. Kennedy's life is honored with a perpetual flame at his burial site at Arlington National Cemetery. It records when the man was assassinated, and the official history tells us who it is presumed pulled the trigger and where. But the details of this crime have long been covered up and disputed. Who hired Oswald? Were others involved? We may never know the answers to these questions and, even if we do, it is unlikely that the answers will be reflected on a public memorial.

I applaud major athletic teams changing names that have offended for years. I am glad that such companies as Quaker Oats and Nestlé are finally dropping commercial brand names that have stereotyped people far too long. But with regard to the statues, I hope we don't erase history in the name of righting historic wrongs. We need to acknowledge our past, fully and in all its complexity. It is the only way we may avoid committing the same crimes in the future. And it is the only way we can know who we truly are.

Removing statues bears an uneasy relationship to censorship and, like censorship, the issue isn't always so clear cut. We deplore a Ku Klux Klan rally, for example, but may support its right to be held because we believe in freedom of expression; and if we prevent the expression of those ideas we hate, we know we may be prevented from expressing our own. On the other hand, some argue that removing offending statues is not a censorship of history (as if history itself were valueless) but rather disqualifies history told in a myopic or prejudiced way. Such memorials were not meant to reflect history but to honor and elevate one side of history over another.

I think of Cuba, where the Revolution has never permitted statues or even portraits of living leaders. During Fidel Castro's life, no public office displayed his photograph, and there were no monuments to him in public places. This was explained as avoiding a cult of personality like those that existed in China or North Korea. A cult of personality always exudes intimidation. Yet intimidation can take many forms, as with the statues of Jefferson Davis and Robert E. Lee throughout the southern United States. Such statues clearly speak differently to Black citizens than to white. The solution, it seems to me, must be tailored to each situation. We know we can only understand a person or event by being willing to listen to all opinions.

But simply listening to others is no longer enough. Our diverse response to the issue of statues and monuments teaches us that the way they affect us depends on who we are, how they make us feel more than what they make us think. It's about emotional empathy. The Victory of Samothrace made me feel strong as a young female child. The pioneer woman made me feel I could overcome all obstacles as an adolescent just coming into womanhood. These were feelings, not social analyses. An African American living in Richmond, Virginia, is going to have an entirely different experience walking past a statue of Robert E. Lee than I or any other white person will have. The African American is forced to confront a tribute to the man who led the army that defended those who owned his great-great-grandparents. Native Americans in California, confronted with a statue celebrating Junipero Serra, are going to feel the pain of the early Christian missions that enslaved their ancestors. Pueblo people in New Mexico know Juan de Oñate as the conquistador who maimed and killed theirs. This is about emotional empathy, something much deeper than political understanding or mouthing the words *I know how you feel.*

There is also the danger that if we remove a statue or change the name of a sports mascot or military base, we run the risk of believing we have dealt with our racism and solved the problem of offensive public displays. These gestures are important, but they are the beginning of a process, not its end.

We must find ways to have an ongoing public conversation about race that include learning empathy. We must explore the role time plays in shaping our cultural values, how different historic moments facilitate different readings of reality. We must look at power, how it is exercised and distributed. Strong religious influences often promote condescension and patronizing attitudes toward specific groups, resulting in some being considered inferior. We need to tear down the statues that offend but make places where they may be displayed with all sides of the story told and room for open discussion about the forces that created them. Only then can we begin the journey toward becoming a nation that feels like home to all.

Our Time Has Come...
with a Few Caveats

U.S. FEMINIST ACTIVIST TARANA BURKE coined the term "Me Too" in 2006. The struggle to raise consciousness got a boost, but the slogan didn't become a movement until January 21, 2017, the day after Donald Trump assumed the U.S. presidency. On that day, more than a million marched in Washington, D.C., and hundreds of thousands in cities across the country, expressing our rejection of a misogynist who reveled publicly in his abuse of women, engaged in racist rhetoric and acts, and spoke derisively of immigrants, calling them rapists and murderers... yet would be our president for the next four years.

We and our allies were raising our voices in opposition to an administration that increasingly showed it would follow hateful words with hateful acts. Then, in October of the same year, #MeToo entered yet another phase. It demanded the focus of names and faces. They weren't simply the brave faces of those women daring to speak out, but also the startled faces of powerful men, men who had freely and flagrantly abused women for years, believing they could get away with their misogynist conduct.

Perhaps more important than the fact that so many of these men are well known is what the movement means for ordinary perpetrators who now have significant reasons to fear discovery. Patriarchy keeps women subservient in order to empower men with a false but exploitable sense of dominance. Most major religions support this inequality, and civic structures have traditionally reinforced it. It is noteworthy that the burden of fear is beginning to shift from the victims who have long been forced to suffer in silence to their victimizers who are being named, charged, and toppled from power.

No longer is a pedophile-riddled Catholic clergy the only or principle target of enraged women and men. And no longer does the general public automatically support the abusers over the abused. #MeToo has begun to change the balance of power in one of patriarchy's most egregious legacies. I want to be absolutely clear: as a feminist, and as a survivor of sexual abuse myself, I applaud the power of this movement that forces us to take human integrity seriously. In my own body, I know how suffering such crimes can shape a life. I know how PTSD feels, how it affects choices and possibilities. A great many well-known men who have long misused their power have been punished. More importantly, a dent has been made in the age-old assumption that all men are naturally and rightfully born into entitlement and women into subordination.

All of a sudden, we are living a new reality. It is incipient and uncertain but beginning to effect change. In some societies, at least, women and girls are now more likely to be believed when we claim we have been abused. Scientific literature is reaching a broader readership. Some police departments have specially trained sexual abuse units. After centuries of trivialization and silencing, our voices are being heard. Institutions are being forced to demote and dismiss executives who for years have sexually assaulted female underlings with the absolute confidence they could get away with their behavior. The mere whisper of sexual misconduct—on social media, in the mass media, or in court documents—is enough to put an end to the careers of men who have long been living confidently above the law.

As with all such movements, especially those attempting to right such historic wrongs, #MeToo's sweep has been implacable. It has crossed borders, taking root in almost every country. And although each country's history and culture shape the movement in different ways, the new consciousness has sent shockwaves through diverse cultures. Women are empowered by our newfound agency. We are rallying and marching by the hundreds of thousands. It has become apparent that we are leading an important revolution, one that looks not only at gender but at the issue of power itself in a holistic way, and that we are combining our demand for gender justice with other struggles: those confronting climate change, poverty, racism, the urgent need for educational and healthcare reform, and a more humane immigration policy.

In this novel situation, the victim is always presumed to be telling the truth. The perpetrator always deserves our repudiation, whether he tells jokes at women's expense and is prone to lewd comments and unwanted touch or routinely rapes and batters. But we must also understand the collateral realities. Values accepted for millennia aren't going to change overnight. Consistent and broad-based reeducation, changes to the law and in the popular perception of what constitutes abuse must all be enforced.

The backlash against change can also be fierce. We have experienced this from the religious right as well as from the Trump administration's validation of certain crimes as evidencing manliness, strength, even patriotism.

Trump is no longer president, but his legacy lives on. As we struggle against traditional examples of abuse, we are forced to take on new manifestations of its underpinnings. This shouldn't intimidate or dissuade us but should encourage us to work harder to effect the change we know is needed, which includes making sure we are advocating for it in a thoughtful way.

Studies show that the sexual abuse offender is usually someone close to the victim: her father, grandfather, brother, uncle, teacher, priest, coach, doctor, or trusted family friend. He is always someone more powerful. According to the U.S. government's Department of Health and Human Services, a source often found to underreport this type of statistic, one in nine girls and one in fifty-three boys experience sexual assault or abuse at the hands of an adult. These numbers are grossly understated. Other sources tell us that one in four girls and one in six boys will be sexually assaulted by the age of eighteen.[1] Eighty-two percent of all victims under eighteen are female. These victims are four times more likely to abuse drugs, four times more likely to experience PTSD as adults, and three times more likely to suffer from depression. According to a study conducted by the National Victim Center, four women aged eighteen and over are raped every three minutes in the United States. This translates to seventy-eight an hour, 1,871 per day, or 683,000 per year.[2]

#MeToo is changing these equations. Where for generations a victim's word was worthless when compared with that of her perpetrator, now it is more often assumed to be true. The victim is innocent unless proven otherwise.

---

[1]. Johnson, I., and Sigler, R. "Forced Sexual Intercourse among Intimates." *Journal of Interpersonal Violence*, 15(1), 2000.

[2]. Kilpatrick, D. J., Edmunds, C. N., and Seymour, A. *Rape in America: A Report to the Nation.* Arlington, VA: National Victim Center, 1992.

The perpetrator is guilty unless—on rare occasions—proved innocent, a turning of the tables that has done immense good for women's self-esteem but has also produced its quota of tragedy.

In this righteous explosion, I want to keep track of the issue of patriarchy itself. How it shapes society, conditioning every one of us from before we are born—males to inhabit a sense of entitlement and females to submit to their unwanted advances, to the extent that they often believe this to be the natural state of affairs, something to be borne in silence, "our cross to bear." The abuser inevitably wields the additional weapon of fear: "Tell, and I will kill you or those you love." A mother will often close her eyes to a husband's violation of a daughter because economic dependence keeps her tethered to such injustice. Too often she herself is also a victim, and thus has been damaged in her ability to understand perpetration and victimization. It may be easier to ignore the evidence before her than to support a child crying out for help. Additionally, young boys who are victims of such abuse often feel isolated and alone; girls and women have the support of a growing recovery movement.

But patriarchy damages men as well as women. It teaches and validates woman abuse, but it erodes the humanity of men. Many of us have said this for decades, since the early days of feminism, yet it has been difficult for us to incorporate this truth into our lives. It is also important to separate the crime from the criminal. The latter can often learn new behavior, sometimes becoming an effective advocate for equality especially among his peers, while the former has long been an accepted cultural norm.

As the Second Wave of feminism took root in the U.S., the dictum "the personal is political" became popular. We mouthed the slogan but were unable to understand its relevance, and we lacked the analytical and emotional tools to apply it to our everyday lives. Now, half a century later, #MeToo is making the connections.

But #MeToo has also made some tragic mistakes. A man might be accused, a victim comes forward with scathing testimony, and in most cases that is enough to condemn the perpetrator. But what of evidence and degree? Should demeaning behavior—unwanted touch, insistent flirtation, belittling discourse, crude humor—carry the same weight as incest and rape? Does a lone verbal insult deserve the same punishment as years of abuse? And what of damaged women who, for whatever reason, exaggerate or lie? We may sympathize with them but lament their targeting someone who doesn't deserve to be singled out. A lifetime of subordination can spark a need for revenge in some who are unbalanced or may really believe they have been wronged.

There are still, of course, the "untouchables," those men who, because they retain an inordinate degree of power, remain at least for now above the law. Politics protects gross offenders, such as Donald Trump, who can brag about raping women, be elected president, and keep the support of half an electorate; Daniel Ortega, who raped his stepdaughter from the age of eleven into adulthood and continues as president of Nicaragua, supported by citizens, women as well as men, who argue that what a man does in his private life should have no bearing on his ability to run a country; or a Supreme Court nominee who has been accused of sexual misconduct but has the support necessary to confirm him to the bench.

I have a male friend who has been accused of making inappropriate or suggestive comments to a female student back in the 1970s. Forty years later, that student, encouraged by #MeToo and also possibly out of a personal imbalance unrelated to the incident in question, accused her former teacher on social media. Other women joined a loud chorus, going so far as to send notes to the man's wife, threatening her with death if she didn't denounce her husband. In the intervening years, this man has contributed brilliantly and generously to his community. When accused, he admitted to inappropriate comments and apologized for the damage he may have inflicted but denied having physically abused his accuser. The student, now a woman, agreed; she had never suggested physical assault. Nevertheless, the vitriol heaped upon this man forced him and his wife from their home of decades, irrevocably changed their lives, and consigned them to an oblivion that robbed us all of their many talents.

Another good friend was an important Latin American singer/songwriter whose work expressed the aspirations and dreams of generations. A year or so after his death, a family member accused him of having sexually abused her sister when she was ten and he twenty-seven, certainly ages when the girl in question would have been an innocent victim and he should have been accountable for his actions. The accused was dead and could not speak for himself. The presumed victim said the incident hadn't happened as it had been portrayed. And the story was being kept alive by a right-wing journalist who seemed intent on ruining the singer/songwriter's reputation. Circumstances that at the very least cast doubt on the story.

I know these men. I acknowledge that they may have engaged in inappropriate behavior; they are, after all, products of patriarchal conditioning. One immediately responded to the accusations against him and then said he would not be drawn into subsequent rehashes. The other is gone and can no longer speak for himself. Whatever their truths, I deeply value the entirety of their lives and believe them capable of reflection and change. I believe that their contributions far outweigh any insult they may have inflicted so many years ago.

There are other cases in which the initial accusations have unraveled, although those accusations cannot be taken back and continue to weigh on the person's reputation. One high-profile example concerns the motion picture director Woody Allen. Allen was accused by the actress Mia Farrow, his ex-wife, of having sexually abused their adopted daughter, Dylan, when she was a child. Despite Allen's denials, his films began to be rejected and his reputation suffered considerable damage. One thing that led people to believe him guilty was the fact that another of the couple's children, Ronan Farrow, carried out in-depth research on the Harvey Weinstein case, resulting in the excellent book *Catch and Kill*. If he believed his sister's accusations, who were we to doubt them? Yet many noted that Dylan's testimony seemed rehearsed. No forensic evidence has ever been proven against Allen. He voluntarily took and passed a polygraph test. It now seems likely that Farrow was using her long-smoldering anger against an ex-husband to ruin his reputation.

The Woody Allen case also raises the question of whether or not we should reject the brilliant work of people whose politics or behavior we may deplore. Even if we believe Allen guilty, do we stop watching his films? We continue to read the poems of admitted anti-Semite Ezra Pound, the writing of avowed fascist Louis-Ferdinand Céline, and the incomparable short stories of arch-conservative Jorge Luis Borges. As indeed I believe we should.

What are we to make of cases in which men have been wrongly accused or the accusations against them exaggerated? In the first place, we must not allow these erroneous accusations to undermine an important movement for social change. When it appears that the accusation is false or exaggerated, we need to look at the life in question, taking every possible variable into account. If a man who has worked for good his entire life is accused of wrongdoing, should we not make room for extenuating circumstances and the possibility of redemption: the nature and extension of the crime of which he is being accused, the evidence supporting the accusation, and his willingness to indulge in self-examination? As a society, do we not possess the tools and sophistication to consider such cases in a balanced way, or must the mob response prevail? Can we not applaud and support #MeToo for the overwhelming justice it brings while recognizing that injustices may sometimes be committed in its name?

I fervently support #MeToo and hope it will reach out and bring down every man whose egregious abuse of women has perpetrated fear, submission, and even death. I harbor no mercy for men—or women—who use their power to abuse others. Much less am I playing the role of devil's advocate. I do ask that in our campaign to right so many wrongs we do not indulge in the same sort of inhumanity we deplore. We must be better than those who wrong us. It is not a question of forgetting, much less forgiving, but of being able to judge by taking the whole person into account. Our decisive but thoughtful discernment can demonstrate that we understand we are in this together. Abuse harms the abuser as well as the abused. To create the world we want and deserve, we need a society that is safe for women and can count on caring men.

Homunculus

PAINTERS IN THE MIDDLE AGES depicted children not as infants but as diminutive versions of adults, the boychild—and it was almost always a boychild—with wrinkled brow who might have been pondering some philosophical or financial concern, his head-to-body relationship that of a fully-grown person. This adult-like child has come to be known as a homunculus, a strange term more fitting perhaps for a malignant growth than for a young person. Some define a homunculus as "an ugly child," attesting to the fact that placing an adult face on a newborn erases the sweet innocence generally associated with infancy.

This has nothing to do with those children about whom one says, "You can see exactly what she will look like when she grows up." No. Those little ones display a facial feature or set of features that bring a whiff of future into the present. An oddly shaped nose or style of eyebrows, a jut of chin or unusually broad brow. The proportions are still those of a child. With the homunculus in medieval painting, the adult head is too small to belong to a newborn. The body is also often muscular: a fully developed physique rather than the folds of baby fat associated with a baby or toddler.

It is believed that this pictorial tradition came from the Christian need to portray the infant Jesus as fully developed, not as some child who might share the physical qualities of any other recently born. The explanation makes sense. It wouldn't be the first or last time Christianity has led us astray. In Europe during the Middle Ages, most portraits were commissioned by the Church, and it stands to reason that such orthodoxy would color all cultural manifestations. As more secular influences took hold, artists were free to experiment more. By the time the Renaissance dawned, it wasn't only the Church but also the Court that commissioned works of art. And artists were increasingly able to give free reign to their desire to paint from life what inspired them, including babies with their natural features and proportions.

But the idea of the fully developed miniature human didn't disappear altogether. It remains in certain examples of folk art and religious iconography in different parts of the world. One of its attributes, in particular, continues to spark my imagination: the image of a small but fully developed person placed inside the image of another's head, no doubt symbolizing the belief that only another brain is able to think our thoughts. It is easy to understand why this belief persisted for centuries, until science rendered it obsolete.

This is different from the folk-art nests of Russian dolls. With them, each doll contains a smaller doll, but each is a complete figure. Not at all the same as one whose head is thinking another's thoughts. Closer, perhaps, to the idea of a homunculus are some of the ancient rock art petroglyphs and pictographs that can be seen throughout the U.S. American Southwest, in which larger human images often contain smaller ones with both clearly representing fully grown adults.

When I see an image within an image, I am reminded of the Dutch Cleanser ad of my childhood, in which a little Dutch girl held a can of cleanser which, in turn, held a little Dutch girl with her can of cleanser, and so forth and so on until the repetitive sequence faded to a mere intimation of continuity. Some images remain in one's consciousness. That advertisement was purely decorative, though, and didn't signify that one little Dutch girl was thinking the thoughts of her larger homologue.

In Mexico in the 1960s, an elderly man from a remote region of the Puebla mountain range lived with us for a few months. He was suffering from tuberculosis of the bone, and we hosted him in order that he see a doctor friend who was only able to make him more comfortable in his final days. Prior to staying with us, Don Rodolfo had never been in an automobile, experienced electricity, or seen any of the other conveniences we take for granted. One night we took him to the movies. He had no explanation for those people walking and talking in the oversized scene before him other than believing that living people had somehow physically entered the screen. In his long life, he had not come in contact with the information that would have permitted him another interpretation.

In some way, out of sync with our more elaborate contemporary systems of thought, those actors were homunculi, in this case larger rather than smaller than the adults they portrayed.

Art has always created its own version of reality. This is one of the qualities that make it art. Cave paintings of bison and other animals rendered forty thousand years ago emphasize movement, which would have been most powerfully present in the scenes those ancient artists conveyed. African masks and other sculptural art exaggerate those qualities—human or divine—most important to their place in the scheme of things. Hindu gods and goddesses are portrayed with multiple arms, symbolic of supernatural powers. Picasso and the cubists dislodged and rearranged the planes of the human face so as to indicate its many angles. Abstractionists are more interested in action than in a static representation of their subjects, while hyperrealists try to paint as much like a photograph as possible. So-called primitive artists privilege certain features because they are most meaningful in terms of the way they see the world. Critics often assume artists paint in a stylized way because they are unschooled or otherwise incapable of rendering a more objective image. I assume they have more meaningful reasons for doing so.

Meanwhile, the homunculus lives on in history and in my imagination: an explanation that has given way beneath the march of time and scientific revelation, but that remains an evocative image whose job may not yet be done.

Becoming Elizabeth Taylor

As a young teen in Albuquerque, New Mexico, I went on Saturdays and Sundays to the Lobo Theater near my house, a small unpretentious movie house my parents allowed me to walk to by myself. I pretended I was under twelve so I could get in for ten cents. But to myself I pretended I was older. I wanted to be a grown and glamorous woman. I wanted to be Elizabeth Taylor.

That little neighborhood theater no longer shows films, instead holding Sunday services for a religious sect that calls itself City on the Hill. Seventy years ago, it was a weekend magnet for me and my friends. After seeing *National Velvet* (1944) or *Little Women* (1949), I *was* Elizabeth Taylor. I walked like her, spoke like her, and held my head just as she did. When others failed to acknowledge my transformation, I waited expectantly, giving them time for recognition. I gazed into the eyes of anyone I met from beneath the long lashes and liquid depth of Elizabeth's violet eyes.

Those violet eyes were the thing. Technicolor had enhanced motion pictures for only a few short years. The very first movie I'd seen was *The Bells of St. Mary's* (1945). Mother took me when I was nine or ten. Ingrid Bergman commanded the screen with her classic beauty. But that picture was in black and white, and I wasn't seduced into becoming Ingrid.

Never, since that magical time, have I so mindlessly embodied another woman. As I matured, I identified much more realistically and profoundly with women whose aspirations more closely resembled mine. Mentors Elaine de Kooning, Laurette Sejourné, and Nancy Macdonald. Heroines Haydée Santamaría and Dora María Téllez. Prophetic poets whose voices still sound in my head, such as Adrienne Rich, Audre Lorde, and Anne Waldman. Rosalind Franklin, the woman who first saw DNA's double helix, although men took the credit and won the big prize and she died at the age of thirty-seven from the radiation in her laboratory. And so many ordinary women who have waged a constant struggle of resistance against patriarchy's obscene demands.

But *identifying with* is not the same as *becoming*. The latter is something you can do only when you are an adolescent yearning to incarnate the unobtainable qualities of your dreams. When young desire holds you in its grip and you are powerless to escape its seduction.

Little Women had captured my young imagination as a novel. By the time I saw the film, I had read the book several times over. I wanted to be Jo, the writer, or maybe the older sister, Meg. But when I saw the film, I *became* Amy, the artist who went to Europe to study and whose life was by far the most exciting. I became Amy because Elizabeth Taylor was Amy, and I had become Elizabeth Taylor.

My young adulthood coincided with Hollywood's era of greatest glory. Judy Garland, Grace Kelly, Marilyn Monroe, and Audrey Hepburn were other magnetic movie icons with whom I grew up. I thrilled to Judy's voice, believed Grace's story of the commoner-turned-fairytale-princess, cried over Marilyn's tragic death, and longed for Audrey's graceful neck. Oh, how I lifted my chin and stretched my neck in an effort to look like Audrey. But none of those personas inhabited me as Elizabeth did.

Elizabeth Taylor in *Cat on a Hot Tin Roof* (1958) or *Cleopatra* (1963) was even more glamorous than she'd been in her earlier films, when she and I were both younger. By then, though, I had stopped emerging from movie houses embodying a star's identity.

I was already beginning to embody my own.

Where Was That Again?

REMEMBER THAT GAME where you spin a terrestrial globe or stand above a spread-out map of the world, close your eyes, and point? Your finger touches down somewhere, hopefully on land rather than in the middle of the ocean, and you have to name and describe the place. This might be a classroom exercise. Or a party game. You could be choosing your next vacation spot, or even where you would like to live. But probably not anything so solemn or lifechanging.

Geography is one of those subjects our schools seem to abandon as unnecessary to modern life. Big mistake. In 1975, I was on a speaking tour of Canada and found myself in Fredericton, New Brunswick. A young Chilean woman attended my lecture. We talked, and she told me that she and her husband had landed there as a result of Pinochet's brutal coup less than two years before. Canada had been welcoming, she said, but in Fredericton no one knew where Chile was, what language was spoken there, or why they'd been banished. She felt as if they had been scooped up and deposited in a place where all links to home had evaporated into thin air.

Imagine how much more at home we might feel in the world if we learned to respect other peoples and their places of origin, and how much more others would respect us. Imagine how much more hospitable we would feel.

We U.S. Americans have been conditioned to believe we live in the greatest country on earth and speak the most reasonable language. When we travel, we too often just talk louder, assuming that's the best way to make ourselves understood. We know few or no other languages when compared with people who come up in other countries. Someone born in a small nation, like the Netherlands for example, probably speaks German, French, and maybe even English along with his or her native Dutch. Many Vietnamese speak French and Chinese as well as their own language. Many South Africans are fluent in English and Afrikaans as well as well as one or two tribal tongues. For natives of Africa and Asia, English has long been a requirement, and today Chinese or Arabic may be as well. We U.S. Americans, though, continue to expect others to learn our language and way of life rather than attempting to meet them on their cultural terms.

This sense that we are the center of the world, if not the universe, is so pervasive that we frequently incorporate it into our humor. I remember the early 1980s, when I lived in Nicaragua. Friends from home would come down to experience the social struggle taking place there at the time. The great African American poet June Jordan visited, and we made some trips together into the countryside. She was interested in hearing people's stories and learning about the Sandinistas' vision for change. One day, in conversation with me, she laughingly referred to Nicaragua as Nigeria. I don't know if the wrong name slipped out or if she used it intentionally to make some poetic or political point. I suspect the latter. But from then on it became a shared private joke; she always referred to Nicaragua as Nigeria. June was deeply sensitive to issues of cultural identity and I understood that she was mocking our well-known U.S. ignorance.

Some place names lend themselves to a perverse humor. Timbuktu is one. Writing this, I have no idea where it is. Bhutan is another; a quick online search tells me it is a remote landlocked kingdom in South Asia that includes happiness when measuring its gross national product. Others place are simply unknown to those of us who have paid little or no attention to other parts of the world. Is Hong Kong a country, or a city in China? Where is little Lichtenstein? I rarely mention Uruguay without someone responding: "You mean Paraguay?" And I cannot forget the moment in 1969 when I tried to send a telegram from Cuba to my parents in New Mexico. The telegraph operator kept assuming I meant old Mexico. It took a full half hour to convince her that New Mexico was one of the U.S. states, albeit stolen from Mexico.

Even here at home, how many people can identify the capital of every state? I wouldn't be surprised if there are many who can't name their own state capital. And then there are places with names that are hard to forget, like Surprise, Arizona, or Truth or Consequences, New Mexico.

This latter town used to go by the much more conventional name of Hot Springs. It was a small, impoverished, and struggling community in the southern part of the state. On March 30, 1950, a popular radio game show launched an essay competition. It called for texts that lauded the virtues of one's hometown. A local from Hot Springs won the contest, and the town's name was changed to Truth or Consequences. The new name brought some attention to the place, which nevertheless continues to be a rather forgotten part of the world. The truth is, the hot springs—rich in invigorating minerals—are reason enough to go there. Despite yearly visits until his death, and despite the fact that the town fathers named a park after him, game show host Ralph Edwards brought few enduring benefits to Truth or Consequences.

Apart from this trivia, colonialism has been the major assault weapon in terms of robbing people of their national borders, land, cultures, languages, security, and ways of life. The Europeans who "discovered" America regarded our indigenous tribes as impediments to conquest. The Native Americans had to resort to treaties—almost all of them ignored or broken—to try to get their own territories back. Many still struggle on vastly reduced reservations. Here in New Mexico, the Spanish land grants are still being disputed by generations of subsequent authorities, and the families that inherited them still contest their claims.

In Latin America, from the fifteenth century on, Europeans—Spanish, Portuguese, Dutch, and French— invaded great kingdoms, destroying centuries-old ways of life developed by the Inca, Maya, and other extraordinary cultures. In the nineteenth century, a few European men of power sat around drinking and blithely divided Africa into client states, with no regard for tribal, cultural, or linguistic differences. Israel's invasion of Palestine has produced generations of death and destruction between peoples who share a common history as well as a common homeland. The bloody Troubles that have come from the struggles between the Republic of Ireland and Northern Ireland can be traced to a similar abuse of religious mandate. The distress that has resulted from these colonialist practices has decimated peoples ever since.

And this arbitrary manipulation of borders didn't end in the nineteenth century. Twentieth-century wars created other divisions that ripped neighbors and even families apart. The separations of North and South Vietnam, North and South Korea, and East and West Germany, as well as other decisions resulting from imperialist policy and the spoils of war, have created untold misery for those who find themselves on one side or another of these fictitious lines. World maps are constantly having to be redrawn to reflect current borders.

President Trump did the same sort of damage by insisting on his wall—the literal one and the metaphorical one, both products of his unjust border policy—between Mexico and the United States. Those parts of the physical wall that went up disrupt the traditional homeland of the Tohono O'odham people who live in southern Arizona and the northern Mexican state of Sonora. It makes life more difficult for residents of the Mexican and U.S. border cities who have always traveled freely to live and work in both nations. It has brought family separations, sent refugees home to face violence and death, and wrenched thousands of children from their parents. And it upsets the wildlife and vegetation that know nothing of vengeful divisions.

Our sociopathic president never missed a chance to punish other nations in subservience to his "America first" mantra. Even such a tragedy as the coronavirus pandemic—or perhaps especially such a tragedy—provided him with an opportunity.

Most history and geography books respond to the interests of those who write them. And they are almost always written by non-natives with particular axes to grind. Most tourist flyers exaggerate a country's best qualities, perfect weather, and exotic culture. Does this mean that we must go somewhere, even live there for a time, to know its positives and negatives? With today's instant access to all sorts of information, it seems as if we could learn about the most remote places and peoples without leaving home.

So, where was that again? It behooves us not only to be able to name all the places in our global community but, perhaps more importantly, to learn something about those places, why they are so unique, and what their peoples have to offer us all.

Mapping Our Lives

FEBRUARY 18, 2020, BROUGHT NEWS of Michael Hertz's death. Hertz was the man responsible for redesigning the New York City subway maps. I'd never heard of him before but, when I lived in that city in the late 1950s and early '60s, I spent untold hours studying the subway maps then in use, straining to see above or around other passengers as the car I rode hurtled along a track and I had to know if I should be making my way toward the door. I was always grateful for their clarity. News of Hertz's mapmaking and death got me thinking about maps in general, their uses and misuses.

The *New York Times* obituary explained that an Italian named Massimo Vignelli had designed new maps for the New York subway in 1972. They were artistically elegant but hard to follow. So, seven years later, Hertz's firm was called upon to improve upon them. It was a group effort. Nobuyuki Siraisi, a Japanese painter and designer working for Hertz, rode every subway line with his eyes closed in order to get a feel for the curves in the routes. Over the years, several architects took credit for those maps, but the *Times* endorsed Hertz's contribution. In death, he finally got his due.

Maps tell us where we are and how to get where we want to go. They are probably as old as writing and art. Cave dwellers mapped stars and constellations with drawings on rock tens of thousands of years ago. The Greeks mapped cities and towns using ink on parchment several hundred years before the Common Era. Most were based on the idea that the world is flat.

In the second century BCE, Eratosthenes, known as the father of geography, was also a mathematician and astronomer, which gave him a more accurate knowledge of spatial dimensions. During his tenure as director of the Library of Alexandria, he wrote a three-volume work titled *Geographika*, in which he described and mapped the entire known world and divided the Earth into five climate zones. Eratosthenes was the first cartographer to consider the world a sphere, and also the first to place grids over his map and use parallels and meridians to link places with one another. His map featured more than four hundred cities and their accurate locations, something that had never been done before.

There is evidence that other nations—China, Babylon, India—have maps dating back millennia. All the great sea explorations were undertaken with the help of maps, some amazingly accurate while others sent ancient seafarers off course to destinations they could not have imagined. When they landed on the shores of what is now North America, fifteenth-century Europeans assumed they had reached India. That's why they called the people they found here Indians. Cartography's errors as well as its certainties shape places and peoples far into the future. And a colonialist mentality continues to define many of the maps we use today.

I was ten when my family moved from the suburbs of New York City to the desert landscape of the U.S. American Southwest. I was fascinated by the land: its space, colors, and seemingly endless possibilities. In adolescence I began buying United States Geological Survey maps, 1:24,000-scale topographic quadrants, also known as 7.5-minute quadrangles. In the half century between 1947 and 1992, the USGS made more than 55,000 of these to cover the forty-eight contiguous states. Similar maps were produced for Alaska, Hawaii, and the U.S. territories.

I remember each quadrangle costing one dollar. I ordered them for the areas of my state I hoped to explore and stored them beneath my bed. I felt as if I were sleeping on a hidden treasure and dreamed about its secrets. The maps were large and unwieldy for a young person such as myself, but I valued them beyond almost anything else I possessed. When I learned to drive, I could get out on my own and, unbeknownst to my parents, explore one of those quadrants, follow its rises and hollows. I walked pieces of the land with a scrutiny I haven't been able to match since. In 2009, the USGS produced an updated quadrangle topographic map series, modeled on the 7.5-minute series but derived from a global imaging system. A new era had arrived.

There are many commercial mapmakers, but most of those that dominate the field—Rand McNally, National Geographic, and the like—base their maps on the Mercator projection, developed by Flemish geographer and cartographer Gerardus Mercator in 1569. The Mercator projection became the navigational standard because it represents all courses of constant bearing as straight segments. Mercator's proportions continue to be used today in road maps as well as maps of the world. It is taught at all educational levels. And it is enormously problematic in terms of how it represents land masses, continents, and nations in relation to one another.

Mercator represents a perfect example of colonialist and imperialist ideology. Europe and the United States are outsized, while the dependent nations are portrayed as much smaller than they are. On a Mercator projection, Greenland appears similar in size to all of South America when, in fact, South America is more than eight times larger than Greenland. Alaska is depicted as roughly the same size as the continental United States. Other land masses nearer the poles, such as Antarctica, are also vastly exaggerated.

To "correct" this misrepresentation, we have the Peters World Map, an Equal Area cylindrical projection with standard parallels at forty-five degrees. It was presented in 1974 at a conference in Germany by Dr. Arno Peters, who claimed he invented it—although well after the discovery of an identical map made by James Gall in the 1800s. I place the word *correct* in quotes because no flat map can accurately simulate a sphere. The Peters map results in a distortion of shape, stretched about the equator and squashed toward the poles, but it has the great advantage that all countries are correct in area in relation to each other. Maps not only represent the world. They shape the way we see and imagine ourselves in it.

Today, AuthaGraph is considered the most accurate map projection available. It is so proportionally perfect, in fact, that it can be folded into a three-dimensional globe. Japanese architect Hajime Narukawa invented the projection in 1999 by equally dividing a spherical surface into ninety-six triangles. Mapping is a complex endeavor, requiring the skills of geographers, mathematicians, and artists, as well as a willingness to depart from traditional colonialist ideas about the world's configuration.

When it comes to mapping and other sciences, the arts are too often overlooked. My wife Barbara is a visual artist who some years back produced a series of collages on paper. She calls the series Personal Cartography. The pieces are alive with a sense of emotional location and journey. Grids and trails intercept images that speak of the land in evocative ways. When I look at her maps, they tell me more about where I am than any more scientifically "accurate" rendering.

Global imaging has changed the way we relate to maps. No longer do drivers depend upon a "navigator," a person sitting in the passenger seat with a paper map in hand. Instead, the car has a global imaging device installed, or travelers use the one in their smartphones. We type in our destination, and a moving map shows us the way. If we wish, a disembodied human voice gives verbal directions as well. Sometimes this voice mispronounces a place name. Sometimes the device thinks we want Greenville, California, instead of Greenville, South Carolina. But despite such quirks that are yet to be ironed out, global imaging represents progress.

It behooves us, however, not to depend too completely on technology. A few years ago, Barbara and I were on a bus rumbling along a dirt road on our way to the Roman site of Butrint in post-Communist Albania. While we took in the scenery, a fellow traveler frantically searched for our position on his personal GPS device. Unable to access Albania, his device was telling him we were nowhere. "We don't exist," he exclaimed anxiously. His dependence on technology had taught him to trust the device over his own experience.

Frequent travelers often stick pins in maps, indicating where they have been or hope to go. There is something satisfying in this, although I fear it also encourages the idea that spending mere hours in a place means a person has "done Rome" or "been to China."

Rest in peace, Michael Hertz. You have left us images as useful as they are beautiful. And you have prompted me to think about what mapping means.

Six Degrees of Separation

SIX DEGREES OF SEPARATION has become a cliché, or at the very least a metaphor, for the idea that chance and science link all humans. We are surrounded by a variety of circumstantial evidence attesting to the fact that we touch one another in ways we may find surprising. The oft-mentioned global village and other versions of "togetherness" as a desirable state pop up at unexpected times and in the least likely of ways.

It might be a film or novel, in which a clever plotline leads us to paths that intersect. It might be the discovery of a skull several million years old that reveals similarities to modern *Homo sapiens*, leading to the conclusion that we developed on different branches of the human tree rather than only one. It might be a personal experience, astonishing and cherished, through which we come upon a connection that sparks our interest or gratitude.

Every so often a thinker, author, or popular culture guru gets us all thinking about how "together" we are.

In today's world, everything from the latest fad in pop psychology to increased population density to Facebook and other social media platforms that can provide us with a thousand "friends" in no time at all constantly reminds us of how close we have become.

The idea of six degrees of separation first gained prominence after World War I, when Hungarian author Frigyes Karinthy published a volume of short stories called *Everything Is Different*. One of the stories was "Chain-Links." Karinthy believed that the modern world was shrinking due to an ever-increasing connectedness among human beings. He posited that, despite great physical distances between peoples across the globe, the growing density of human networks made the actual social distances shorter. This was long before the internet, with all its social media sites. And long before COVID-19, when social distancing became a safety measure.

The characters in Karinthy's story began to discuss this idea and:

> ... a fascinating game grew out of this discussion. One of us suggested performing the following experiment to prove that the peoples of the earth are closer together than they have ever been ... We would select any person from the 1.5 billion inhabitants of the Earth—anyone, anywhere at all. He bet us that, using no more than five individuals, one of whom is a personal acquaintance, he could contact the selected individual using nothing except the network of personal acquaintance.

Karinthy is regarded as the originator of the notion of six degrees of separation. That notion, in turn, impacted the related idea of three degrees of influence, which deals with the quality of such connections rather than simply their existence. From then on, mathematicians, sociologists, physicists, and others have continued to expand what has come to be known as network theory. As with so many theories that find their way into popular discourse, this one may be regarded as either a fun idea or a scientific field.

Yet despite the apparent shrinkage of modern-day life, ideologically we have never been more separate. Class, race, gender, culture, dislocation, age, mental and physical abilities, religious and political beliefs, and disparate educational opportunities and access to food, shelter, and healthcare divide us irremediably, often brutally. Forced exile and great migrations uproot peoples from their natural habitats, creating disruptions of language, custom, and wellbeing. Although the so-called social issue differences have become more familiar in recent years—how we identify sexually, our religious beliefs or cultural manifestations—they still trigger large-scale bullying and hate crimes. I am talking about people being made to feel othered, the very antithesis of connection.

Although we have now had an African American president and recently had a major-party Mormon nominee, these identities remain uncomfortable in mainstream U.S. society. While president, Obama received hundreds of times more death threats than any previous occupant of his office. Ugly, racially motivated derision was outrageous and widespread, and those who engaged in it seemed to feel entitled. When Hillary Clinton ran for president in 2016, a great deal of the campaigning against her focused on her gender, in ways both crass and subtle. And then we had a president who modeled and encouraged misogyny, racism, xenophobia, and hate speech of all stripes, never missing an opportunity to divide rather than unite people. What's worse, he provoked his followers to echo, and often act upon, those sentiments, something many of them are still doing now that he is no longer in the White House.

As long as citizens in the top economic bracket luxuriate at the world's most expensive spas even as members of the middle class are forced into homeless shelters and the poor go hungry, the idea of six degrees of separation acquires farcical characteristics. We may be connected genealogically but are more and more separate in the ways that matter most. For the privileged, gated communities hold the multitudes at bay. For a Black youth such as Trayvon Martin, even a gated community offers no protection against murder at the hands of a man who believes he is entitled to kill out of fear of the Other.

The six-degrees-of-separation phenomenon nurtures an interest in genealogy and has produced a number of popular television programs. *Roots*, the TV miniseries based on Alex Haley's 1976 novel of the same name, riveted audiences fascinated by the idea that African American families could trace their heritage all the way back to their African origins. *The Genealogy Road Show*, *Family Historian*, and *Who Do You Think You Are?* are more recent productions in this ever-more-popular reality show genre.

Progress in crystallography and biology is also to be noted. Gene therapy promises cures to many serious illnesses and conditions, and those who consider its potential to be the next great leap in medicine and those who object to the necessary experimentation on religious grounds continue to fight over its use or abuse.

The relatively new science of DNA has acquitted innocent prisoners (including many who spent half their lives on death row and, tragically, many who were executed before they could be cleared of crimes they didn't commit). It has reunited stolen grandchildren with grief-stricken grandparents in Latin America's Southern Cone. It has also enabled the family members of the disappeared in Guatemala and elsewhere to identify the remains of loved ones murdered and tossed into unmarked graves.

Some genealogy projects have less laudable aims. The Church of Jesus Christ of Latter-day Saints (the Mormon church) has used its excellent genealogical database, one of the most complete in the world, to identify those murdered during the Jewish Holocaust and baptize their "souls" into the Mormon faith, making easy "converts" while enraging Jews who rightly consider the practice to be insolent in the extreme. Needless to say, bridging degrees of separation can be a tool for any interest. It all depends on who makes the connection, and to what end.

I am more interested in exploring the social and psychological connections that place us close to or distant from our neighbors than I am in researching the science or attacking the pseudoscience. We belong, after all, to the human family. Why do we need a parlor game to acknowledge this?

On the other hand, the idea that blood is thicker than water does seem to express feelings that go beyond the purely relational. Cultural differences come into play here as well. Some people would give a kidney or their life for a family member. Others would do so for anyone. Still others wonder how they could have been born into a family in which they feel so alien.

In this respect, South America's Southern Cone has been the scene of great turmoil in recent years. As the grandparents and grandchildren who were victims of the Dirty Wars of the 1970s reconnect through the DNA bank established by Argentina's Mothers of the Plaza de Mayo, some in the younger generation must grapple with the fact that they have grown up in the homes of those who murdered their biological parents or were complicit in their deaths. Some have resisted turning against those they always considered to be their parents. In others, resentment and rage have been almost too much to bear.

I am appalled by the ignorance and exclusivity that has kept one worthy effort for social justice separate from others. When will those struggling for economic justice realize their fight is intimately linked with the struggles for racial, gender, and LGBTQ justice? When will those suffering from the crimes of corporate greed or governmental warmongering understand that incest, rape, and other forms of so-called domestic violence are but more intimate examples of the same sort of power abuse gone rogue?[1] When will those pushing for immigration reform link other social justice issues to their own? And when will all these groups come to understand that without environmental justice, we are all doomed?

I believe that this unwillingness to understand how what oppresses one oppresses all was at the root of many of our twentieth-century failures to achieve social change. If we were Marxists, we prioritized class. If we were feminists, we focused on gender. If we saw change as possible only within the individual, we emphasized one or more version of spirituality. If we thought only a healthy body capable of motivating healthy social interaction, we put our energies into fitness programs and holistic practices. All these traditions have something to offer. But extreme sectarianism kept us from listening to one another. Each group claimed there would be time to consider the needs of others once victory was theirs. That time never came.

Each group's victory inevitably assigns another to the hell at the bottom of the social pyramid. It is as if we must

---

1. This is considered an irrelevant issue for those who support Daniel Ortega, the current president of Nicaragua. Ortega was one of the original Sandinistas and continues to identify as such. Even after it came to light that he sexually abused his stepdaughter for nineteen years, many supporters claim that is "personal" and has nothing to do with his qualities as a political leader. I find this argument absurd.

target someone to be the repository of our ignorance and fear, and in so doing attempt to build ourselves up. Today, that most targeted of all groups is composed of transgender people, and to an even greater extent those who identify as intersex (individuals who were assigned a sex at birth, almost always male, and have grown up with a socially imposed identity they do not recognize). Just because such people are beginning to speak out, becoming visible at the fringes of our exclusionary social compact, does not mean that we have made room for them. They are ostracized, bullied, imprisoned, or murdered daily.

If only six degrees of separation or fewer stand between each human on our planet, it should follow that we understand that what oppresses, endangers, bullies, or betrays one of us oppresses, endangers, bullies, and betrays us all. And from this understanding should follow an understanding of our coexistence with animals, plants, oceans, and air.

Six degrees of separation is an intriguing pastime or food for a few moments of carefree thought. It's when we translate it into daily living that it becomes more serious. Then we are called upon to put socially conditioned fears and biases aside, and to contemplate the beautiful consequences waiting when we breach divisions built of fear.

Calling Paulo Freire[1]

PAULO FREIRE'S GROUNDBREAKING BOOK, *Pedagogy of the Oppressed*, appeared in English in 1970. It linked education to culture and changed my thinking about education itself. If we conceive of the Sixties as I do—that is, as stretching from the late 1950s through around 1975—we immediately understand how that book informed our struggles for justice and equality at a time when social activists believed we could successfully challenge oppression and do away with exploitation.

Those were heady times. *Pedagogy of the Oppressed*, along with other revolutionary texts, such as Franz Fanon's *The Wretched of the Earth* (1961) and Benjamin Spock's *Baby and*

---

[1]. Excerpted and revised from a virtual talk delivered upon receipt of Chapman University's Democratic Project Paulo Freire Award, July 7, 2020. I am humbled and honored to have received this award: first, because Freire's thought has been so important to my own evolving social analysis; and second, because of Freire's great relevance for today.

Child Care (originally published in 1946 but comforting vast numbers of young mothers in the 1960s), joined *The Communist Manifesto*, Mao's *Little Red Book*, and Che Guevara's *Man and Socialism in Cuba*, giving us new ways to think about inequality and liberation.

As a young single mother in 1960, I would have been lost without Spock's commonsense approach to childcare. Without Fanon and Freire and a host of other innovative thinkers, my world would have been much narrower, circumscribed by the conformity and hypocrisy of the times. In the United States, the 1950s had catapulted Senator Joseph McCarthy to sinister power and produced the hearings before which so many citizens were called to incriminate themselves and others. The majority refused and were imprisoned, lost jobs, were vilified for years after. The anticommunist witch hunt, which was really an assault on anyone with progressive ideas, limited respect for difference and freedom of thought. Its chill lasted decades.

For a young girl just coming into what was to be my own creative work, the restrictions emanating from this right-wing ambush were even more severe. Men returning from World War II had forced middle-class white women back into the domestic sphere (already and still the working domain of many Black women), and capitalism was busy inventing enticements so that we would feel that's where we wanted to be. I graduated high school in 1954, and it may surprise you to learn that back then girls my age weren't encouraged to study either science or mathematics in U.S. public schools. It wasn't until three years later, when the Soviets launched Sputnik, the first successful manmade satellite, that our educational system started training female students in a way it hoped would help the country to catch up. Access to those areas of knowledge for us was not about equality but about global competition.

The radical difference between the ideas put forth by Fanon, Freire, and Spock and those of the Eastern philosophies and homegrown self-help movements which then also began to gain adepts, especially among the more affluent, was that the former saw problems as socially determined. Solutions would take class, race, and eventually gender and other social variables into account. Religious and New Age gurus preached individual fixes, alleging that only after fixing ourselves could we fix society. More importantly, the spiritual routes demanded faith, while the scientific formulae offered reason-based evidence of how they could work. And movements with gurus at the top are dependent on vertical structures, recreating authoritarian systems that are exploitative by nature.

In the past decades, we have seen a dramatic increase in the climate crisis, a breakdown of capitalist social organization, a worldwide pandemic, a violent surge in police brutality against people of color, and neo-fascist administrations in the United States and several other countries. We have also recently witnessed powerful grassroots organizing that connects all these issues simultaneously and seems determined to protest them until change is achieved. Great masses of people are acting out of a perfect storm of frustration and rage. In this context, Paulo Freire's ideas take on a powerful relevance.

Control of any population begins with control of public education. In the United States, we can see how decades of intentionally obliterating progressive educational strategies has produced generations of students forced to memorize and excel at multiple-choice testing rather than develop the capacity for critical thought. Long before No Child Left Behind, and up to and including Betsy DeVos's elitist privatized vision, the U.S. educational system increasingly produced conformist citizens unable to challenge even those policies that negatively affect their own lives. These generations of poorly educated people account for many of those who voted Donald Trump into office and continued to support him despite his outrageous, frequently criminal, behavior. Given this, the powerful energy of sustained antiracist protest during Trump's final year in office was all the more remarkable.

Freire believed that the very nature of the teacher/student relationship was skewed. When teachers are considered the authority and students are expected to parrot their ideas and instructions, he wrote, real learning cannot happen. Freire saw authentic dialogue as an act of love, humility, and faith. Dialogue gives people the independence to experience the world and name it accordingly.

These ideas were soon adopted by Second Wave feminists who first engaged in consciousness-raising groups and later—in academic settings—rearranged classroom configurations and broke with traditional professor/student dynamics. A whole new learning experience led to more democratic ways of sparking intellectual curiosity, encouraging exploration, and effecting social change.

One of the offshoots of this movement was a new way of thinking about language. Over the past several years, people of all genders have begun to follow their names and titles with their preferred pronouns, ranging from the old *she* or *he* to *they* and other choices, thus recognizing the needs and rights of trans and intersex people. We no longer allow others to name us. We do not refer to the homeless, but to those without homes; we don't say people are disabled, but that they have a disability.

It is to the credit of the millions of young people protesting today that they are able to break from conservative conditioning and challenge a national security state with all its greed-based, consumerist, classist, racist, sexist, homophobic, and xenophobic underpinnings.

Occupy, the grassroots members of the Bernie Sanders campaign, Black Lives Matter, #MeToo, and a number of other movements have broken with the verticality of political parties and other top-down groups. This has allowed for more, and more diverse, voices to be heard, the most oppressed among us to demand justice, monuments honoring oppressive politics to come down, some changes to police tactics to be made, and no few abusive men to be charged with and convicted for their crimes against women. This lack of verticality, while more spontaneous and inclusive, also makes organizing for change more difficult because it is not connected to lawmaking and choosing our political leadership. It remains to be seen how this issue will be resolved.

Paulo Freire believed that the central problem of humanity was that people were unable to affirm their full human identities. He conceded that each of us strives for humanity, but oppression interrupts our journey—clearly much more dramatically for the poor and marginalized. Dehumanization is tantamount to objectification. Freire understood that when the oppressed fight for opportunity, they can easily become oppressors themselves.

We can see this when we look at the ways in which Israel invades Palestinian land and rights. Or how our European pioneer ancestors fought the Native Americans and imported Africans who were forced to become property working the southern plantations. We have inherited a racist society. African Americans, especially, have been dehumanized in this country from the moment they were kidnapped and brought here as slaves. Neither Emancipation, Civil Rights, nor subsequent gains really set them free. Segregation, lynching, Jim Crow, sustained exploitation and oppression, mass incarceration, and living constantly as targets of extreme racism have taken an unspeakable toll. Today's police violence only puts this situation front and center once again. Native Americans, Hispanics, Asian

Americans, and other minority populations have similar stories of historic grief.

Freire also cautioned against the oppressors "helping" the oppressed, false solutions we have seen play themselves out in such failed programs as the Peace Corps, Alliance for Progress, Christian missions, and international banks trapping poor nations in unsustainable debt. Here at home, too many white liberals claim to know how people of color and the poor feel, a sentiment which, however well-intentioned, is a slap in the face to those suffering institutional and individual discrimination.

Freire insisted that we not speak for the oppressed but listen to them. Listening is woefully absent in today's interactions: among individuals, social groups, and on the part of those passing themselves off as our leaders. Freire argued that to truly understand oppression and exploitation we must live like the oppressed, experiencing what they experience. Although in practice this may not always be realistic or possible, there are certainly ways in which we can better approach attempts at mutual understanding. In the wake of so many recent national traumas, the absence of an honest, in-depth, and inclusive public conversation has clearly prevented us from understanding one another and seeking viable solutions to our collective problems. The failure to hold such a conversation has only increased authoritarianism and the oppression of the most vulnerable.

What is imperialist expansionist war, if not the most extreme example of not listening to the Other?

In the last chapter of *Pedagogy of the Oppressed*, Freire laid out a road map for how the oppressed can truly liberate themselves. He explained that oppressors employ what he called anti-dialogical actions, and the oppressed must develop dialogical actions to fight them. He defined anti-dialogical actions as including conquest, manipulation, divide-and-rule, and cultural invasion. He defined dialogical actions as including unity, compassion, organization, and cultural synthesis.

Freire's 1960s ideas are a guideline upon which we, drawing upon our own more recent experience, can build. As history unfolds, we gain new insights. Those of us involved in the national liberation struggles of the last half of the twentieth century remember how revolutionary movements often used unity as an excuse to ignore the needs of entire groups. When I lived in Cuba during the 1970s, the antiracist struggle and a necessary gender analysis were both sacrificed to the perception that nothing must be allowed to get in the way of a unified front against the imperialist threat. Cultural synthesis has also proven to be an ambiguous goal. Today we can see how honoring and respecting a variety of cultural expressions is a better way of reaping what is most valuable in each.

Since Paulo Freire's brilliant work, more recent philosophers, poets, and social activists have given us their own analyses. And previous thinkers have become more relevant. In addition to Paulo Freire, I acknowledge profound debts to Socrates, Galileo, Karl and Jenny Marx, Wilhelm Reich, Walter Benjamin, Elaine de Kooning, Martin Luther King, Jr., Che Guevara, James Baldwin, Audre Lorde, Haydée Santamaría, Adrienne Rich, Mark Behr, and Lucy Lippard, among others. Some of these men and women have given us original visions, sending us in entirely new directions. Others have cast old ideas in a new light. The most brilliant enable us to look to our own experience, trust intuition and imagination, and build upon their ideas to make philosophical contributions of our own.

Today we are trying to survive within overlapping systems of oppression and corruption that threaten to obliterate human life. Excessive use of fossil fuel has brought about a degree of global warming already melting polar ice caps, raising sea levels, causing monster storms, and killing millions. The governments of those nations producing the greatest amounts of CO_2 refuse to take responsibility for the destruction they cause. Food industries no longer simply feed; they have become multi-billion-dollar operations that slaughter animals inhumanely. Corporations genetically manipulate seeds, and farmers commit suicide at higher rates because their harvests no longer produce the bounty they have known for generations. Additionally, the coronavirus pandemic and subsequent economic collapse in many countries have produced or intensified widespread hunger and famine. Advanced capitalism is less and less capable of meeting human need.

In the United States, intensifying police violence and strongarm methods have been responsible for more in a long list of murders motivated by racial hatred and the sense, on the part of cops, that they can get away with them. Most of the victims of these crimes are Black men, most of their victimizers white. It is a gross understatement to say that racism is out of control. Black Lives Matter quickly rose to the occasion. Protests against such violence on the part of law enforcement quickly spread, bringing hundreds of thousands into the streets and challenging police tactics. Just a year ago, football players who took a knee during the playing of our national anthem in protest of this country's unchallenged racism were vilified. Today, those who remain standing are the ones who must explain themselves.

Around the world, millions are marching in solidarity with us. This rebellion is different from so many in recent years: more widespread, more decisive and persistent, stronger, and buoyed by a rage that will not be silenced. And all this started happening on the watch of a narcissistic, sociopathic, and fascistic president. Despite decades of systematic destruction of critical thought, people haven't lost their ability to rebel.

We need Paulo Freire as never before.

Land

WHEN I THINK ABOUT LAND, it's the U.S. American Southwest that comes to mind: the high desert and deep canyons that were familiar throughout my teenage years when place became indelibly embedded in my consciousness. In midlife I returned to that landscape. I understood that I needed it for my emotional and physical health, for my life accompaniment, and for my poetry. As a child and adolescent, I had mostly experienced this land through the window of a car. As a returnee, I learned to explore it on foot, hike its mountain trails, hold my breath before its ancient ancestral sites and rock art. And life brought me a woman who loves this land as I do.

Ancient sites and rock art are one with this land, evidence of the lives of those who have gone before, who lived with its idiosyncrasies and difficulties as we of today no longer must. Thousands of years ago, this region looked different than it does now. It may have been wetter or drier, more tropical or colder, more dramatically affected by the elements. The people who lived here then were shaped by its whims in ways that would do us in. The sites and rock drawings they left behind hold this knowledge for us.

Engraved in sandstone, molded by wind and sand and water, is a history the high desert asks us to remember, depositing only the lightest of footprints, taking only its stories to keep and pass on. To meet the land on equal footing, we must slow way down. Time has its own tempo and temperature here, as it does everywhere.

The rainwater collected in hollows in the rock, called *tinajas* (earthenware vessels), holds tiny shrimp-like animals with sixteen-day lifecycles, and if a *tinaja* dries up before the cycle is complete, they don't die but go into stasis. When it rains again, they finish out their cycles, no matter how many days remain. In this magical calendar, my footsteps go in tandem with my breath. My eyes are able to take in vast spaces and the smallest change in the texture of stone. I listen for the voices that spoke here so long ago, and sometimes I hear them.

Those voices whisper the desert's secrets. Its contradictions confound those who don't inhabit its landscape. It says *dry*, while beneath a brilliant sky it sometimes sends an attack blast of water rushing through a slot canyon, destroying everything in its path. Water becomes mud. Unsuspecting hikers become corpses. And not a cloud to be seen. On the very same day, if someone traversing its distances isn't carrying enough water, dehydration and death wait around the next bend. A flash flood and the agony of thirst are complementary enemies.

The colors of this land comprise a palette I can see with my eyes closed. Mauves. Orange reds. A thousand shades of beige and brown. The pale green of lichen, the gray-green of sage, and the bright green of rabbit brush. Fuchsia flowers on the outstretched arms of the cholla and the pale yellow of a prickly pear bloom or brilliant red of a claret cup. The forever blue of sky. Cryptobiotic soil holds a key to the future, and I must be careful not to destroy it by stepping on its rich brown loam. Such footprints can remain for decades. The temperature of this place is hot, pulsing, fierce.

Shimmying up a narrow crack in the rock to emerge atop the mesa at Chaco Canyon, I look down on Pueblo Bonito. Its hundreds of rooms, dozens of kivas, and partially remaining walls are like a full-size model telling me about its period of most vibrant occupancy. Closer to Albuquerque, ascending from the narrow slot canyon at Tent Rocks and gazing from above upon formations shaped by centuries of weather, I breathe the land in all its solitary beauty.

Near Moab, Utah, where wind and water have carved the sandstone into arches and bridges, a drawing on a boulder in the middle of a field depicts a scene of childbirth recognizable in any era. The mother's legs are spread; the child has emerged; both figures are surrounded by oversized drops: blood or maybe tears. I touch its lines and feel the presence of a woman who lived hundreds of years before my time. This image, engraved on the rock so many centuries before, connects us.

My own Sandia Mountains, so named because they glow like the sweet inner flesh of a watermelon as the sun sets each afternoon, challenge me from the moment of my return. La Luz trail rises from their base at seven thousand feet to its high point at ten. It takes me more than a year to climb that trail, from its desert beginning through several ecosystems to the top. Each time I attempt the feat, I am able to go a little bit farther. Once I picnic at a midpoint and watch fascinated as two climbers scale a nearby rock face. On that evening's news I learn that, despite being expert climbers, two doctors fell to their deaths that day.

On La Luz I observe my strong legs in wonder. In high school I hated gym class, wasn't attracted to any of the team sports, performed them so poorly that I was always the last one chosen when the captains made their picks. How could I have known that my sport was in my body all along? When I reach the top, and then repeat the climb again and again, I feel as if I own the land.

But that's precisely what one cannot do: own this land. Its power lies in its resistance to being possessed, or even less, conquered. I suspect that those who claim they have "done all twenty-thousand-foot peaks" or "conquered the world's highest mountains" have a very different relationship to land than I have. Not worse or better, just different.

I cannot claim this land, yet it claims me. Arizona's Grand Canyon is interwoven with all Barbara's and my years together. It is both vast and intimate. I have also gone there with my parents, all my children, and several of our grandchildren. I have walked along its rim, hiked into its depths, and traveled its river more than once in a little wooden dory, sleeping on its small beaches and exploring some of its side canyons. More than any other place in this part of the country, Grand Canyon displays every desert color, from deepest purples to rich reds and creams. When Barbara and I fell in love, we drove over to that canyon to buy our first commitment rings.

This land, the high desert, is where I find myself.

Disaster's False Dichotomy

WE DIFFERENTIATE BETWEEN HUMAN-MADE DISASTERS and those caused by nature. But this is a false, and ultimately misleading, distinction.

If a building housing sweatshops collapses in Savar, Bangladesh, killing more than a thousand workers, we blame the architect who approved the plans (undoubtedly for monetary gain) and a government that cannot establish building codes or, if they exist, refuses to enforce them (plenty of kickbacks there as well). We can blame the clothing brands in the U.S. and other Western countries that reap exaggerated profit and have rarely been serious about improving the working conditions under which their clothing is made. They know that real remedies would only add to their overhead. Concerned citizens, sick and tired of trying to get those multi-billion-dollar companies to take responsibility, can even reproach the individuals who purchase the clothes. There's plenty of blame to go around.

Similarly, when a mine tunnel caves in, we blame the mining conglomerate that year after year refused to deal with complaints about unsafe conditions and a lack of safety measures. Sometimes such disasters provide an opportunity for the very people at fault to garner some good publicity through a series of actions designed to appear heroic once an accident has taken place. Miners die, but CEOs can console their families and pretend to offer help.

Such was the case, at least for a while, when on August 5, 2010, a tunnel caved in eleven hundred feet below ground at the San José copper and gold mine at Copiapó on the Chilean altiplano. Thirty-three men were trapped inside. For seventeen days, no one on the surface knew if the men were still alive. Then a rescue detail heard a faint tapping down below, and a note with the words "33 alive" was attached to the end of a rope and raised to the surface. As tension mounted, a second tunnel collapsed. Across the globe, the drama caught people's attention. Engineers put their creativity to the test, and one came up with a way of digging a borehole to where the men waited for what they imagined could only be a slow and painful death.

Chile's conservative president, Sebastián Piñera, certainly contributed to this mining disaster, and others. His own family owned profitable mines, and his government consistently refused to improve conditions for the miners. But during the ordeal at Copiapó, Piñera turned the situation to his advantage, staying at the site and in full view of international TV cameras, comforting the families, and promising his government would spare nothing in its effort to rescue the men.

At a makeshift tent city, inhabitants were telling stories reported in newspapers around the world. These were the stories of wives and children enduring an agonizing wait. And then, amazingly, mining experts, engineers, and others put their heads together. They dug a tunnel, constructed a capsule just large enough for a single human body, and dropped it through that tunnel. One by one, all thirty-three miners were brought to the surface. Those most responsible for causing such a disaster basked in the glory of the mission accomplished. No doubt this was a heroic event. I still remember sitting up that whole last night watching a live stream of the men being brought out.

But no sooner than the news reports had faded, the tenor of the story changed. The rescued men were alive, but most were unable to work, many had psychological problems, none received adequate health care, and a number were wracked by severe PTSD. Television shows, even in the U.S., spotlighted their story. But, once the accident had faded from the news, no one in the Chilean government cared what happened to the victims or their families.

Soon, as always, the next compelling event captured our attention. A year later, few of the miners had been able to return to mining. Fewer still had secured other jobs. Their lives and the lives of their families had been destroyed. And Chile itself wasn't any closer to legislating better mining conditions. President Piñera had achieved his fifteen minutes of fame, and thirty-three heroic men had lost nearly everything but their lives.

This is the way it turns out with most of these humanmade disasters that can be traced to negligence or greed. The responsible parties have the money and influence to bend other people's tragedies to their advantage. Perhaps the most outrageous recent example of this right here in the United States is the British Petroleum Company's Deepwater Horizon oil spill.

On April 20, 2010, an explosion destroyed the Deepwater Horizon, one of BP's drilling platforms off the coast of Louisiana in the Gulf of Mexico. Eleven men lost their lives. But that tragic loss of life was not the end of the disaster. For eighty-four days, it proved impossible to cap the resultant oil leak, which continued spewing crude and saturating the waters of the gulf at the rate of hundreds of thousands of tons a day. The viscous coating strangled wildlife, clogged shoreline swamps, and severely affected a number of coastal industries, from fishing to tourism.

Every government oversight agency promised to make BP clean up the mess, and the company promised it would. To judge from its ongoing TV advertising, it would "stay until the cleanup is complete" and "no one cares more about the people of the Gulf than BP." Less than a year after the spill, the company boasted that the area's fishing and tourism industries were back at pre-spill levels.

But let's look at some statistics BP would prefer we ignore. The greatest impact was on marine species. The spill area once hosted 8,332 of these. They have largely been decimated. During a January 2013 flyover, former NASA physicist Bonny Schumaker noted a dearth of marine life in a radius thirty to fifty miles around the well. Much farther afield, photographs of pelicans dying beneath a coat of crude provided one of those images that can pack such a wallop. A definitive link has been established between the death of the Gulf's coral community and the spill.

People, too, continue to suffer. Aside from thousands of lost livelihoods, by the June following the explosion 143 exposure cases had been reported to the Louisiana Department of Health and Hospitals; 108 of these involved workers in the cleanup efforts, but many were reported by ordinary citizens who just happened to live in the affected area. Chemicals from the oil and dispersant are believed to be the cause of the illnesses. Mike Robicheux, a Louisiana physician who treats people who have been exposed to toxic chemicals, has described it as the biggest public health crisis from a chemical poisoning in the country's history.

After the accident, the area experienced a marked increase in mental disorders and stress-related health issues.

Environmental scientist Wilma Subra reported finding amounts of volatile organic compounds five to ten times greater than safety thresholds in those people coming in with oil-related illnesses. If past experience is an indicator, however, we have probably only seen the tip of the iceberg. Problems linked to the Deepwater Horizon explosion will likely continue to be felt generations into the future.

The economic impact on the people of the Gulf Coast has been severe. On the one hand, residue from the spill continues to affect seafood, fishing, and tourism. On the other, Louisiana's local officials fear the offshore drilling moratorium imposed in response to the spill will further harm the economies of coastal communities. The oil industry employs about fifty-eight thousand Louisiana residents and has created another 260,000 oil-related jobs, accounting for about 17% of all jobs in the state. As with every such situation, a way must be found to balance the need for employment with serious environmental concerns.

Following the BP disaster, public opinion polls in the U.S. were generally critical of the way President Obama and the federal government handled the disaster, and extremely critical of the company's response. British Petroleum says it's there for the long haul. But as of March 2012, the company estimated its total spill-related expenses hadn't exceeded $37.2 billion, yet it listed its 2012 profits alone as $25 billion. Perhaps more troubling is the fact that BP and other big oil companies continue to ravage the Mississippi and Louisiana Gulf Coast. There are stretches where, as far as the eye can see, a poorly regulated oil industry is making the land its own. We have a history of such tragedies followed by vows to pass legislation that would eliminate them going forward, only to be followed by political jockeying that makes regulatory change impossible.

All of the above is but one illustration of the point that distinguishing between so-called natural disasters and those considered humanmade is a false dichotomy. Humans are increasingly responsible for climate, weather, industrial, and war-provoked disasters. Humans with power are the most responsible of all—not only for the disasters themselves, but for the impact they have on others.

It is no coincidence that the most impoverished and vulnerable among us are the most likely to suffer when a mine tunnel caves in, a sweatshop collapses, a landscape goes up in flames, or an oil rig explodes. Only nature produces earthquakes, you may say. But that's like the National Rifle Association's claim that it's only bad people who cause the shootings that have wracked our schools and malls, not their guns.

No event in recent times has demonstrated more dramatically than the COVID-19 pandemic the tenuous line between a disaster that seemed natural in origin and the carelessness or disregard with which we humans managed such a disaster. As the coronavirus made its way across the globe, human decisions determined who was hit hardest, where most people sickened and died, and how derivative damage affected communities, businesses, and general wellbeing. Countries whose governments stepped up to provide help did better than countries whose governments didn't. The experience was entirely different for a wealthy family that could move away for a while than it was for those living in crowded tenements, nursing homes, or prisons. Those with access to efficient medical attention had much better survival rates than those who couldn't even get into hospitals.

Who allows communities to be built on known fault lines? Toxic waste dumps are never situated in wealthy neighborhoods, but where poor children play and poor families drink the water. Contaminated groundwater invades residential areas unable to fight back. Even such "natural" disasters as earthquakes and tornadoes affect many more poor people than those with the money to construct well-built homes in safer places, or whose children are able to attend schools with shelters.

Some disasters happen because there is a perfect storm of heat and cold, drought and wind, conflicting air currents, or a fault line that doesn't hold. Some can be more easily traced to human greed: the mineshafts without safety features, the oil rigs at which officials turn their backs when they should listen to warnings of impending problems, the factories lacking even the most elemental safety conditions.

We call some of these tragedies human-made and others natural. But what is the difference, when the same people are the ones getting hurt?

Our Little Secret

IT'S OUR LITTLE SECRET.

No one but us would understand.

Who do you think would believe you, anyway?

If you tell, I'll kill you.

If you tell, I'll kill the people you love most.

Just one more time, I promise.

You know you like it.

You know you want it.

Our little secret.

Do these or similar pleadings or threats sound familiar? Do you remember someone saying one of these things to you as a child or adolescent? Do you remember what they did to you before they said it? Did you believe them? Were you so filled with revulsion or fear that you didn't know what to believe? Or was the act pleasurable in some uncomfortable way, the shared secret making you feel special for a while, and for years after ashamed of feeling that way?

Power plays by its own rules. It often wears an invisibility cloak as it targets its victims and grooms them to acquiesce—or at least, conditions them not to tell. When someone with power abuses us and then shrouds the act in secrecy, something only to be shared between the perpetrator and the victim, it is as if we've been assaulted twice: once in the act itself, and again in the trap of being unable to ask for help, to share the weight of the abuse. Too many who do manage to ask for help are not believed.

Shame is one of power's most insidious weapons. It is the weapon that makes this second assault possible. Our societies conjure shame in order to shift the blame from the person committing the crime to the victim, and to keep the victim beholden. Our perpetrators use our shame to make us feel the abuse was our fault. We wanted it. We asked for it. We encouraged it, somehow, by giving off the wrong signals, wearing the wrong clothes, saying the wrong thing, exhibiting the wrong demeanor. Maybe we even liked it—and are embarrassed to admit it. Keeping it a secret is the only way we can swallow our shame—and, of course, protect the perpetrator.

Shame is always accompanied by fear, another weapon that keeps us silent.

And, just as the incessant repetition of a lie can make it seem like the truth, repeated abuse can feel like it is something we deserve, that it's our fault.

Abuse comes in a variety of forms—psychological, intellectual, physical, sexual; often all in the same package. Young children may believe it's just the way things are. If the assault is something we experience repeatedly, we become accustomed and tend to believe our abuser. Maybe I could have stopped it early on. Maybe I could have told someone who would have believed me. Maybe this happens in all families; it's just that no one talks about it. He is my father, after all. Or my grandfather, my brother, a trusted family friend. I know he loves me. It must be my fault.

As long as I don't divulge the secret, it will be all right.

I was an infant when my maternal grandfather sexually abused me as my maternal grandmother watched. I didn't yet have the power of speech. Although the abuse itself weaves in and out of memory, it is stored in my cells. Sometimes, even today, I can see my grandfather's steely eyes and my grandmother's slack-mouthed hunger. I don't know if or how I showed my repulsion. Perhaps I was confused. Perhaps I tried to resist in some infantile way. Perhaps I lay passive, waiting for it to end. Perhaps I disassociated. At that tender age there was nothing I could have done that would have kept the incest from happening.

It took almost half a century for me to retrieve the memories in a psychotherapy session, and to link a phobia I've had for as long as I can remember to my grandparents' incestuous behavior. I've been able to understand that phobia a bit better, but it continues to have a powerful grip on me. My grandparents have been gone for decades.

Abuse is always about power. Powerful men (and they are most often men) feel entitled to use powerless women and children (boys as well as girls) to satisfy their needs. And such needs have nothing to do with sexual satisfaction. They are about confirming their own power, to themselves and to others. They are about patriarchy, the millennia-old system that privileges male superiority, male entitlement, men having their way with women and children and governments and whole groups of peoples and ideas, in secret if necessary. Male entitlement is rampant among men everywhere, and it crosses all class, racial, and cultural lines.

Abuse is not limited to domestic relationships, and it's not just individual abusers who keep their victims in the dark, demanding their silence. Powerful nations invade and exploit smaller, less powerful ones. Institutions manipulate their members. Mega corporations exploit and abuse their employees, clients, and customers. The Catholic Church has for generations allowed priests and other members of the hierarchy to abuse their congregants, many of them adolescents and children. Thousands of victims have been sacrificed to protect the institution. And, although this abuse has been exposed most broadly in Catholicism, it exists in every faith.

In 1954, the U.S. Central Intelligence Agency overthrew the democratically elected government of Guatemala. In 1973, it did the same in Chile. These were not the first nor the last times the CIA managed to engineer such coups. I think of Iran, Indonesia, and most recently Bolivia. All were carried out in utter secrecy. It took whistleblowers and researchers a long time to unearth and publish the top-secret agency documents that prove these crimes. The information always came much too late to prevent the takeover or save the victims.

There have been a few notable exceptions. During the U.S. American War in Vietnam, Daniel Ellsberg dared to copy and publish the Pentagon Papers. Revelations concerning the real history of that conflict and its coverup by successive administrations empowered an anti-war movement strong enough to help end it. But most such information is released long after the fact, when the damage has been done and even most of those culpable have died or received immunity. Ellsberg would not be able to do what he did back then in the current political climate. In the United States today, such courageous voices are criminalized.

It took years of congressional effort to force the tobacco company executives to admit to the deadly effects of smoking. I can still see them, sitting in a tense row before the congressional committee, forced to tell the secret they had kept for generations. The tobacco companies were fined, though never as much as they had racked up in profits while they made their customers ill and caused their deaths. They had to add warning labels to cigarette packs.

There was a time in American political life when such redress was possible. But before these secrets were revealed, the U.S. spy agency, military, and greed-based companies made billions in profit and hundreds of thousands of people died. Today, whistleblowers are fired and sometimes even imprisoned.

Abusers always depend on secrets to further their schemes, whether they are a father abusing his daughter, a priest abusing a parishioner, a corporation abusing its employees, big business abusing the public, or an imperialist power abusing a nation within its sphere of influence.

The secrets do us in, the little secrets and the big ones. They do not keep us safe but make us more vulnerable, whether we're talking about children being abused by their elders, women being abused by the men who claim to have their best interests at heart, smokers who believed the tobacco company executives who told them for years there was no proof that smoking was bad for their health, citizens kept in the dark about all manner of policy affecting our lives, or voters who believe that austerity and other neoliberal measures are good for us.

Secrets only benefit those who are doing something wrong, something they don't want others to know about.

The next time someone asks, "Can you keep a secret?" you might consider answering: "I don't traffic in arms." If only in solidarity with those for whom secrets have been lethal.

I Told You
It Wouldn't End Well

EACH YEAR, THE FLU SEASON SPREADS FEAR along with a new crop of viruses, some of which will retreat when faced with the current recommended vaccine, some of which will find a way to kill. Thousands of people will succumb. Some of us dutifully get our flu shot. Some scoff: "Oh, I never bother with that." The flu doesn't discriminate.

If it's a particularly virulent strain—influenza, avian flu, SARS, or something similarly unexpected and brutal—the deaths may rise to the tens or hundreds of thousands. Perhaps even the millions. We're always waiting but never prepared for the really devastating attack, something like the plague that swept across Asia, Europe, and Africa in the fourteenth century, killing fifty million people. Or the influenza pandemic of 1918. The latter was so severe in the United States that it depressed life expectancy by ten years.

As I write, we face COVID-19, caused by a form of coronavirus. The World Health Organization has just designated this new virus a pandemic. It has quickly become a worldwide crisis, affecting human health and the global economy. The coronavirus likely originated in Wuhan, a city of eight million most of us had never heard of, and quickly spread worldwide. The Italian government, caught off guard, eventually shut down the entire country in an effort to contain the disease. Parts of Japan were quarantined, and soon other nations followed. Everywhere, travel and large public events were canceled, schools and universities closed.

Our biochemists try to stay ahead of the game, but we know that any really lethal and widespread pandemic could wipe out a large fraction of humanity. Such is the risk of living at a time when we fail to deal with the care of air, water, and foodstuffs, when we have been foolish about almost every preventative health measure, overused antibiotics, and assumed that pandemics will be a problem for the future, not for us.

To help cope, some may indulge in a bit of dark humor. The 1918 epidemic produced some of that. More innocent and carefree than adults, children that year are said to have skipped rope to the rhyme:

> I had a little bird.
> Its name was Enza.
> I opened the window,
> and in-flu-enza.

Those who lost family and friends weren't amused by such levity. For the victims of a pandemic and their loved ones, no sort of humor or play is appropriate.

Many modern-day pandemics originate in China. I'm not sure why. Perhaps because it is such a large country with so many people. Perhaps because safety precautions aren't as stringent there. But we fool ourselves if we believe they are stringent here. Whatever the reason, we can always expect a racist response, and not only toward the Chinese but toward anyone who looks Asian. A friend who teaches at a New York City college tells me several students there were attacked because they are Asian. In the U.S., especially, we are prone to giving free rein to our racist impulses.

China used to be a country we thought of as mysterious and remote. Today, it surpasses the United States in economic influence, and even the most ignorant among us must take it into account. China also surpasses us in solidarity. During the coronavirus outbreak, after China contained the situation at home, it sent a plane with medical equipment and specialized personnel to Italy, where the entire country was shut down by the disease.

The coronavirus problem reminds me of another pandemic, just as contagious in its way. For as long as I can remember, we've suffered from an illness that is philosophical and emotional rather than physical. Cynicism is its name. It is a sort of deeply rooted pessimism, a suspicion, mistrust, or negativity so pervasive that whomever is infected cannot help but see the worst in any situation. What good has been promised can't possibly happen, they reason, and if it does it will turn out to be worse than we can imagine. Such world-weary minds are capable of bringing disenchantment by virtue of how sure they are that disaster is just around the corner. Armageddon Christians fall into this category. So do politicians who sow fear to help their electoral chances, and others whose childhoods were so painful and frightening that they were left with no alternative but to expect the worst in every situation.

Flu pandemics are visible. Invasions of cynicism are invisible, and destructive in a different way.

We live in a world where cynicism shouldn't surprise us. Greed and a rampant abuse of power prevent progress in solving problems like war, hunger, human displacement, and the proliferation of illnesses once thought to be eradicated. Watching our so-called leaders at work may turn the most optimistic among us to pessimism. It's important to remember that this is what the crooked politicians want. If they can submerge us in despair, it will be easier to keep us in line. Which is why it's important to defuse or, better yet, defeat a cynical outlook.

I had a grandmother who was a master of negativity. If she couldn't find peril in a situation, she would invent it. When you accidentally spilled something on a blouse or skirt, her first words were: "You know, that will never come out." If you blew your nose, she predicted pneumonia. Even if you spoke about a happy event, she could always predict disaster.

I remember traveling by train one summer from New York to Maine with my mother and her mother—this cynical grandmother. I was six or seven and excited about sleeping in our compartment's upper berth. My dream was dashed when my grandmother mandated: "Absolutely not. She could fall out in her sleep and break her neck." Today, I can imagine how personally unhappy she must have been to have nurtured such an attitude. Back then, I simply resented it.

Cynicism is not to be confused with irony, an entirely harmless expression that uses language normally signifying the opposite for humorous or emphatic effect. Cynicism is a character trait, irony an affect. Sarcasm, mockery, and satire are frequent components of irony. Used well, they can be entertaining, even instructional. Like cynicism, the idea of irony began with the Greeks. It was a device used in Greek tragic theater; the full significance of a character's words was clear to the audience, while the character uttering them appeared not to have a clue. But while irony can enliven a situation, cynicism destroys it.

Cynics believe the world is doomed. Those who engage in irony believe that by pointing out dire situations they are making human interaction more interesting. Unlike the journey of infectious disease, cynics can change course if they want to do so. One's attitude is a choice. I've learned in my own life that it's possible to make different choices even at an advanced age.

It's past time we urge the cynics among us to turn all that negative energy into everyday acts of resistance and solidarity, from a gentle hello to positive feedback when people demonstrate ideas for change and to forcefully opposing the criminal policies that are robbing us of our future.

Naming Ourselves

As a writer, someone for whom words are currency, I am interested in how we name ourselves, others, and the things around us. Few phrases annoy me more than the oft-repeated "they say." Who is that "they" we quote so carelessly? Such unmindful attribution is, I believe, at the root of our society's easy acceptance of the claims made in so much commercial advertising. Too often the phrase "studies show" refers to studies financed by the very companies selling the product involved, without acknowledging the obvious conflict of interests.

One of the things that happens under fascism is that certain words are not permitted; if one is caught uttering them, it can result in being fired from one's job, imprisoned, or worse. A careful reading of history tells us that lists of words were off-limits in Nazi Germany and under other authoritarian regimes. The Trump administration also frequently restricted language. Someone present at a 2020 Centers for Disease Control meeting about the coronavirus reported that words such as *vulnerable, entitlement, fetus, evidence-based,* and *science-based*—among others—were prohibited when speaking about the pandemic. Insisting upon words that truthfully represent us is as important as resisting such imposed restrictions in our use of language.

The time in which we live and the language usage and nuances that are part of our evolving culture inform the way we name. How we named ourselves became particularly important in the 1970s in the United States: *Chicano/a, Latino/a, African American, Native American, Indian, rebel, feminist,* and so forth. Today we can add *queer, nonbinary, trans,* and *Latinx* to the list. Some of the terms we have invented for ourselves reflect healthy political choices. But beware. In adopting some we may unwittingly be pandering to colonialist or other negative definitions of personhood. One example of this was when the term *Anasazi* fell into disuse because it means "enemy to the Navajo people." The term *Ancestral Puebloan* replaced it, but *Puebloan* is from the Spanish, the very people who invaded and conquered so many tribes. I haven't heard much discussion of that contradiction.

In the last half of the past century, we also became conscious of the fabricated value placed on marriage; feminist women began refusing to use *Miss* and *Mrs.* In their place we invented the neutral *Ms.* In the 1970s, when I lived in Cuba, *compañero* and *compañera* gained currency, indicating anyone who was a colleague, friend, or even life partner. Sadly, the custom has faded in recent years. A recent poem of mine reflects the change, paying tribute to a language innovation whose loss I mourn:

When Justice Felt at Home

Something has changed.
Only old friends,
those who shared split peas
and white rice
on sweltering Havana nights
still call me *compañera*:
sweet designation
meaning comrade or friend
lover or familiar
in those luminous days
when justice felt at home
in our desire.

Now, more often than not,
it's *señora*:
regression to a prehistory
when married or single
young or old
mattered most.

Still, *compañera* and *compañero*
are indelibly embossed
on the swaying trunks of Royal Palms,
in Sierra Maestra granite
and along the dissembling coastline
of an Island that still shouts freedom
into gale-force winds.

Today people who do not want to subscribe to the old binary designations—*he* and *she*—have taken how they want to be addressed by others to a much more complex level. They have coined entirely new pronouns such as a singular *they/them* and *zi/hir*. In academic settings, people frequently list their preferred pronouns after their name. Linguistically, I find I have trouble ascribing the plural *they* to a single person. At the same time, I appreciate a determined resistance to the absurd assumption that we can be acceptably only male or female. The arc of who we are is obviously so much more nuanced and individual.

As a deeper understanding of who we are produces an ever-changing consciousness and sensibility, this self-naming goes through changes. Names such as *faggot, lezzie, kike, spinster, gimp,* and others, hateful in the mouths of those who would use them to denigrate us, have sometimes been retrieved, reimagined, and turned on end when used by those who have been their targets. For example, in certain situations African Americans may call themselves or another African American *nigger* and it means something entirely different from when that epithet is used by someone of another race. *Dyke* has been reclaimed by some butch lesbians. A heavy woman may proudly call herself *fat* when the word on someone else's lips is an insult.

In recent years, even mainstream society has become more conscious of the racist and misogynist language used in commercial advertising and popular song lyrics. Public discussion has come from a number of philosophical stances and has ranged from patronizing to illuminating.

Back to Cuba. During the early years of that country's revolution, we all said *we* rather than *I* when speaking in the first person singular. This was an attempt to identify with, or speak for, some vague proletariat, and in retrospect I find it naive and embarrassing. When feminism came along, I became conscious of the way my culture said *mankind* or *men* when we meant *humankind* or *people*. I began to incorporate gender consciousness into my speech.

Since Spanish is a gendered language to begin with, this was more complicated in Spain and Latin America than in the U.S., but feminists in those parts of the world quickly found creative ways to do away with linguistic gender bias. More recently, when wanting to eliminate male assumption in written Spanish, Latin Americans have taken to using *x* or @, a visual combination of the feminine and masculine pronouns, as a way of indicating a gender-neutral ending to nouns that traditionally end in -*a* (feminine) or -*o* (masculine).

Throughout my lifetime, how feminist women speak about ourselves has become more conscious and intentional. We no longer say we were abused, raped, battered (the passive tense implying an act that simply happened, free of a perpetrator—or even somehow casting the victim as responsible). We have learned to say: "so-and-so abused me," "so-and-so raped me," "so-and-so battered me"—or harassed, exploited, demeaned, or bullied. We have learned to assign accountability in language, the first step in demanding redress. Similarly, we are not disabled but a person with a disability, not crazy but someone suffering from a mental illness, not homeless but someone (perhaps temporarily) without a home. In other words, we refuse to be defined by a condition that describes only one part of who we are or a temporary situation in which we find ourselves.

How we are named—literally the name given to us by our parents when we were born or adopted by us later—can have important implications for our lives. I speak from experience. Before I came into this world, my mother gave birth to an older sister who lived only a few hours. Her name was Margaret. Mother became pregnant with me soon after losing her first child; she often said she felt she'd carried me for eighteen months, thus conflating the two pregnancies. And she named me Margaret as well.

I like my name but have sometimes felt as if I usurped the identity of a sister I never knew. My full name is Margaret Jo. The Jo was not, as it turned out, after one of the sisters—the writer—in *Little Women*, a favorite book of my youth, but after Josephine Lehman Davidson, the maternal grandmother I always disliked and who I would much later in life realize had looked on as my maternal grandfather sexually abused me when I was an infant.

As a teenager, I began going by the name of Meg. I wanted to pretend I had been named for Meg and Jo, my two favorite sisters in the *Little Women* clan. No amount of pretending, though, could reconcile my given names with the characters in that book. Like it or not, I was named after my dead older sister and a grandmother I detested. People who knew me at an earlier period in my life sometimes still call me Meg. And through all my years in Latin America I never became Margarita. Now I am simply Margaret again, a name with which I have come to identify.

My last name, too, has gone through some dramatic changes. I was born Margaret Reinthal, the only one of my siblings to have had my father's surname before he and Mother changed it to Randall. Somewhere I have a copy of my birth certificate with Reinthal crossed out and Randall inserted in its place. Having borne a Jewish last name with parents who so obviously wanted to erase all Jewishness from their identity produced a determined response in me as well. I spent years trying to get my mother and father to admit the real reason for changing our name. I knew but wanted to hear them say it. And I, alone among my siblings, and in spite of not being in any way religious, held on to characteristics I hoped defied what I felt was my parents' duplicity.

When I married for the first time, and in line with the custom of those times, I took my husband's last name, becoming Margaret Jacobs. When we divorced, I remember having to pay one hundred dollars to reinstate Randall. When I married Sergio Mondragón in Mexico, I became Margaret Randall de Mondragón. According to the Spanish custom, wives were *de* or "of" their husbands, literally property, at least in name. After Sergio and I separated, I never again took a spouse's surname. From then on, I remained Margaret Randall. Barbara and I have been together for thirty-four years but have never thought about blending or taking one another's names. We remain individuals who love one another.

What we call ourselves may be less important than what we do. But what we call ourselves also informs what we do. When we understand the historical context in which a photographer preferred to call herself a tradesman rather than an artist (Dorothea Lange), a woman artist preferred to be seen simply as an artist without the gendered adjective (most female artists of the past century), or a poet refused the label *poetess*, we claim identities that more accurately reflect who we are.

I tell myself and others: pay attention! Demand that language, in whatever medium, does not minimize, misidentify, confuse, hurt, shame, bully, or kill.

Makeover

MAKEOVERS ARE VALUED IN OUR SOCIETY. There are so many ways a woman, especially, can fall short of whatever beauty standard is currently in vogue. She can be too fat, too short or tall, have too big a nose, or eyes that are the wrong shape. She can have the wrong hair, which usually means too short or frizzy, or the wrong way of dressing, which may mean too masculine or out of step with current fashion. These conditions are socially devalued, causing the woman herself to be devalued by all those who follow the latest industry tips and who would like to believe themselves to be in the majority.

But there are fixes. Most are expensive, but some can be done at home. All you have to do is pay attention: to magazine stories with titles like "Lose Fifteen Pounds in Ten Days," "Look Years Younger," "Release the Inner You," or "Start Over Again at 65." There are depilatories and skin creams, nail polishes and lipsticks. There are permanents and hair straighteners, both guaranteed to ruin your hair eventually but both multi-million-dollar businesses.

There are TV shows devoted to full-body makeovers. The victim (i.e., the chosen one) appears at the beginning of the hour, pale and morose, slouched and resigned, wearing a sweatshirt three sizes too large and pedal-pushers over scuffed loafers. She looks as if she would rather be anywhere except on that stage, and her visible shame tells us she is fully aware that she is to blame for her inferior look. But the team that will do the makeover is exuberantly confident. To a suggestive swell of music, they lead the woman from the audience's sight.

Just before the show is over, and after at least seven commercial interruptions for beauty products of all kinds, the curtains part once more. We are about to witness a miracle. Now the music is rousing, anticipatory. Usually, the woman's husband or children are on hand; their shrieks of "oh my god" and "I can't believe what I'm seeing" are guaranteed to enliven the show's climax. The woman appears, smiles shyly, manages a few model-like gestures, and turns full circle so we may better appreciate what has been accomplished.

The slimming lines and attractive colors of her new outfit hide unsightly bulges and make her look thinner and younger. Her new hairdo, amazingly involving both coloring and stylish cut in such a brief time, takes at least twenty years off her appearance. She is standing straight: always helpful in situations such as this one. The husband runs to embrace and kiss his wife, careful to turn toward the cameras and fight back tears as he exclaims: "This is the woman I married." The children say they've wanted to see their mom looking like this for years. No one mentions the load of housework that will still be demanded of the woman, or how she will be able to keep up her new beauty routine while continuing to fulfill her wifely and motherly roles.

None of these fixes are sustainable. Like most mass-media sleight-of-hand, they depend on a dozen unseen tricks of the trade. Still, such shows earn top ratings. All women are conditioned to believe we need a man in our lives and that we will only be appealing to that man if we are thin, perky, and fashionable. All men are conditioned to desire this sort of woman.

Coming of age in the conservative 1950s, I nonetheless resisted society's stereotypical messages about women. I remember my mother's promise that I would be able to "get my nose fixed" when I was older, and my rejection of that promise. It no doubt helped that I moved in artists' circles. Levi's and a shirt were my standard dress. I wore my hair long, sometimes pulled back in a ponytail or into a bun. In Mexico, I favored the bright huipiles or embroidered blouses worn by indigenous women in that country and in Guatemala.

It was in Mexico, probably in 1966 or thereabouts, that I had my one and only makeover. We had lots of visitors, artists and writers who came from many parts of the globe, attracted by the bilingual literary quarterly I and my husband of those years founded and co-edited throughout the decade. One of those visitors—I will call her The Poet—was a woman who, contrary to most of her sisters in the trade, teased her hair and wore makeup worthy of the work of professional beauticians.

Only an hour or so into the visit, she offered me a makeover. My initial impulse was thanks but no thanks. But she was persuasive, and I was curious. Why not, I thought. And with that, she and I retired to the second floor where, she claimed, my transformation wouldn't take long. I cannot remember the details of her machinations. They must have included some sort of makeup base, lipstick, eye liner, and shadow. I do remember The Poet's enthusiasm as she worked. It was as if she had been given a full palette and a blank canvas.

And I remember descending the stairs to the living room once more and showing myself off. My young son, Gregory, who must have been six or seven at the time, took one look at me and burst into tears. "Where's my mommy?" he cried.

I raced back upstairs and took vigorously to my face with a wet washcloth. As quickly as possible, I scrubbed the lie away. That was the last time I disfigured myself in such a way. My friendship with The Poet cooled after that. I'd always known that I disliked the makeup and fashion industries that coax (one might go so far as to say coerce) women to spend millions in order to conform to a particular look. But now I had experienced that deception in my own flesh.

My young son's tears were a powerful reprimand.

Today, in my eighties, I contend with another challenge. It has to do with how I want to show myself in photographs. As a writer, I am often asked to produce a head shot to grace the back cover of a book or accompany an interview. I have always found women who use photos that show themselves twenty or thirty years younger than they are to be disappointing representatives of my gender. After all, I've reasoned, we should be proud of the evidence of aging that our experience has bestowed.

But there is a difference between an image that shows the natural beauty of maturity and one that reveals every sagging wrinkle, every unwanted hair and mottled age spot. Recently, I have been faced with the choice: do I use a publicity shot that shows me as I was a few years back, when the initial signs of age showed in my face but I could still be considered a handsome older woman, or one taken today in which the beginnings of a full beard cover my cheeks and my face is a mask of undeniable decay?

    I hope I will always be willing to show myself as I am, with all the telltale changes with which my years have endowed me.

The Age of Lies

IF THERE IS HUMAN LIFE one hundred years from now, and analysts refer to our time, it may well be dubbed the Age of Lies, after the Age of Enlightenment or the Age of Reason. Or, like the eras in the mist of prehistory, the Cretaceous or the Jurassic, they may call it the Period of Lies. For this to happen, those analysts would have to retain some understanding of what constitutes truth and how to sort the misleading definitions from what really was. This may be difficult because lies beget lies and the habit of truth is (sometimes permanently) eroded.

Even today, as we read or listen to descriptions of our lives that we know are patently untrue, even as we inhabit an utterly different reality than the ones falsely depicted, our actions too often demonstrate a tendency to believe what is said or written about us rather than trusting and defending our own experience.

From the distance of time, an appraisal will be more difficult.

One important thing to understand about lies is that power perpetrates and protects them. When power is curbed, we have far fewer lies.

Let's look at some examples. I will limit myself to the United States, although it is clear that this society is not unique in its ability to deceive. Take such a basic issue as income inequality. There's the well-worn lie that anyone who works hard can succeed. If you're poor, it is because you are lazy. These days, even the once-middle class knows this is not true. And in the United States, most of us call ourselves middle class.

Literally every minute the obscenely wealthy have more and the poor less. By 2016, the world's richest one percent had more than the remaining ninety-nine percent. But we don't need statistics (too often taken out of context or misrepresentations themselves) to show us what is happening. The pain is palpable.

Every politician promises to fix this injustice in some way or another, and almost all of them lie when elucidating their positions. Those on the left offer exuberant promises; how many times have you received an email in your inbox claiming "McConnell Out!" as if the Himmler of the Senate had already been defeated—or would be with one tiny financial donation from you? The right has no shame about piling lies upon lies. Those who aspire to political office promise to create jobs, punish some corporations deemed "too big to fail," redesign our tax system or close its obvious loopholes, attract business, or any one of a dozen other proposals. Those who show themselves to be dismissive of the poor are criticized by most of us, those with the most inclusive rhetoric applauded. Meanwhile, income disparity grows, and the jobs that are created pay less and come with fewer benefits. Only 3.8% of American workers are unionized today, and a thousand schemes cover up the fact that the rich continue to stockpile money to the detriment of those whose labor creates it. The COVID-19 crisis has thrown the world into health and economic turmoil like few of us have seen in our lifetimes. It remains to be seen what lies this crisis leaves in its wake.

Almost every politician, irrespective of the political party to which they belong, devises clever ways of talking about these problems. Every one of them promises change but fails to mention that change will only come about if a majority in Congress votes for it and the president signs it into law. Once in office, campaign promises are forgotten, and the nature of the U.S. political structure makes compliance all but impossible. The lies have unfolded bit by bit, until the public doesn't know who or what to believe.

Within this panorama, all sorts of subsidiary inequities continue to exist and deepen. Women earn eighty-one cents for every dollar made by a man, and our "invisible" labor in the home remains unpaid. Minority populations (some of which will soon be majority) continue to earn less and have more restricted access to higher-level positions. COVID-19 has exploded these figures; as I write in December 2020, thirty million U.S. workers have lost their jobs.

Public education becomes poorer, and outlandishly expensive private schools train new generations of moneyed leaders, who learn to lie with much greater sophistication. Those most affected often vote for those whose policies are least concerned with their interests—because the lies are presented with such conviction. And the lies continue to accrue. Have you ever wondered why Social Security is called an entitlement, when it is money that we ourselves have earned throughout our working lives and which has been subtracted from our paychecks?

Complicated studies, statistics, polls, and advertising campaigns weave a fabric that is convincing but dishonest. No wonder so many are disinterested in voting, when flagrant lies, voter intimidation, gerrymandering, and obscene amounts of money so often determine the outcome of our elections.

Another area rife with lies is the population's health and wellbeing. The truth is the United States has two healthcare programs that have generally proven their efficacy over the years: Medicare and the Veterans Health Administration. Both have problems; both could be streamlined and improved. But rather than model a system of universal healthcare on one of these largely successful plans, we have allowed our fabricated fear of "socialized" medicine and our pandering to insurance and pharmaceutical companies to keep us on the profit-making track. Simply extending Medicare to every citizen, beginning at birth, would do the trick. We could pay for universal coverage by eliminating the overly complicated for-profit system in place today, with its mountain of paperwork and ample opportunity for graft. The COVID-19 crisis laid bare the terrible inequities in our healthcare system. As always, those at the bottom (doctors, nurses, orderlies, retired healthcare professionals) have stepped in heroically to try to save lives.

How to educate our children has descended into a similar morass of cover-up and deception. Following George W. Bush's ill-conceived No Child Left Behind Act, we hoped a new administration would seriously address a situation that has our nation ranking lower each year in its ability to teach its youngest members to think. But an over-emphasis on testing continues to hobble our educational system. During the Trump administration, we suffered a governing clique that intentionally kept our children uneducated. There is a great deal of damage to be undone.

National security has become another dangerous catchall for far too many political lies. Fear is absolutely the best way of keeping the lies afloat. The messages alternate: one moment there is "credible proof" of a new attack about to be unleashed, the next we are told not to worry;

the illegal observation and search-and-seizure to which we are subject is keeping us safe. A state of continual tension, laced with racist profiling and a new tolerance for the use of lethal force on the part of our guardians of law and order, produces nothing more nor less than bedlam, continuous war, illegal torture, collateral damage that no longer shocks a battered public sensibility, and a false sense of security. A largely hidden digital invasion of every aspect of our lives has rendered us more and more vulnerable to a lying system.

The lies become easier, more acceptable, more embedded in the national psyche.

Art exposes the lies a system perpetrates. In art—music, poetry, theater, the visual arts—we can often find truths that government officials would prefer we do not know.

What we have needed, since long before 9/11, is an honest, in-depth conversation about America's role in the world, the ways in which our country has actually given birth to and armed some of the forces now aligned against us, and how a change of policy might lead to sustainable peace. We need an honest assessment of our own war crimes, even as we pontificate against those committed by others. Many nations—South Africa, Chile, Guatemala, Uruguay, Argentina, Peru, Bosnia, and Rwanda among them—have established peace and reconciliation commissions or tried those charged with atrocities. These efforts have allowed people to begin to replace the lies with truth. The United States needs to embark upon such a journey. Without it, memory cannot be made whole.

Human beings everywhere want the same things: freedom, peace, dignity, work, food, shelter, health, a future. The first step on the road to these is truth: identifying the perpetrators (giving them first and last names, as sexual abuse survivors have learned to do), allowing the victimized to speak, and rewriting the Official Story. Only human exchange, on a level playing field, can make this dream reality. For the United States, only humility and self-examination, not its ongoing bully stance, must be realistic first steps.

But humility and self-examination don't go with the web of lies. And today an even bigger, more urgent issue demands our attention: global climate change and the rapid depletion of necessary resources such as clean water, food, and air. Without a sustainable planet, income inequality, inadequate healthcare, broken education, even the ravages of violence and war, all take second place.

Governments and international organizations have been talking about climate change for decades. But with rare exceptions, the issue has functioned as a political football more than an undeniable threat. Science clearly shows that human-produced carbon emissions are increasing the earth's temperature, melting ice caps, causing mega-storms, and raising sea levels to alarming degrees.

In most discussions, the powerful are privileged and feel entitled. But despite their belief that their children and grandchildren will somehow escape a doomsday scenario, the powerful are as vulnerable in the long run as the powerless. The former will be able to hold out a bit longer. The latter will suffer first. We are talking about losing humanity here, and also about what humanity has produced: art and literature, music, scientific advances, knowledge, and mystery. And we are talking about every animal, insect, and tree.

The stakes have never been higher.

And the lies have never been more expertly woven. So-called impartiality is the watchword of our time. Climate change deniers are given a place at the table alongside the scientists whose research warns of imminent danger; the myth of equal representation allows the lie of doubt to linger. Protecting power has become the mantra by which we live. The poor and disenfranchised are expendable.

A single lie, if well-constructed, often proves difficult to walk back. A web of lies, conceived, produced, and sustained by the most powerful governmental, military, and corporate structures known to history, is much more complex and can be much more difficult to expose.

But not impossible.

Dictatorial or authoritarian leaders, for a time all-powerful, have been defeated. Think of Hitler, Stalin, Pol Pot, Pinochet, Cheney, or Trump. Small armies of brave resisters sacrificed everything to a cause they knew was urgent. Resisters attracted resisters. Good won over evil, truth over the lie.

Authoritarian political systems have crumbled. The Catholic Church, with its untouchable Vatican, long condoned and protected an all-powerful hierarchy, the abuse of women and children, and a code of law aimed at controlling great numbers of the faithful. A few courageous voices, many of them belonging to those very women and children, initiated a struggle against the lie and today hold out hope for millions.

Throughout the world today, women are standing up for gender equality. The #MeToo movement has gone viral, demanding accountability from men who routinely use and abuse women simply because they feel entitled to do so. The year in which I am writing this, 2020, showed women's fierce determination in massive marches and rallies on International Women's Day, March 8. And in Mexico, on March 9, women staged a Lysistrata-type protest by refusing to leave their homes. Millions remained inside, not even using social media. They are estimated to have cost the country well over a billion dollars. They were protesting the femicide that murders ten Mexican women a day.

We are witnessing a slow, uneven, but sure dismantling of criminal practice.

In all areas of human endeavor, determined thinkers and doers use education, organization, constitutional law, well-reasoned argument, and a truth that is easily recognizable to break through the façade of lies.

At the beginning of this piece I evoked an Age or Period of Lies, like the Age of Reason or the Jurassic Period. In times of extreme trauma, those who choose integrity are often motivated, at least in part, by thinking about how they will be able to answer when their children ask them what they did when the great lie threatened life. What will be said about our era if we are not able, as a people, to stand up to those who are destroying us?

Cultural anthropologist Margaret Mead (1901–1978) said: "Never doubt that a small group of thoughtful, committed citizens can change the world; indeed, it's the only thing that ever has." Change happens when someone and then many decide enough is enough and take the first step. Change happens when someone dares to point out that the emperor isn't wearing anything. And others notice—perhaps a few at first, then many, and then many more.

Was Shakespeare a Political Poet?

I'VE NEVER HEARD IT SAID OF SHAKESPEARE that he was a political poet or wrote protest theater. It was simply appreciated in his day, as it continues to be in ours, that the great bard had a talent for creating characters, presenting situations, and telling stories that reflect life's central dilemmas and joys: love, fear, death, jealousy, taboos, and the struggle to be true to one's beliefs. And that he exercised those skills marvelously. His vast output, mastery of the language, and skill in taking on the issues of the day—which turn out to be the issues of all days—make his work enduring.

In most parts of the world, good writing that movingly depicts the battles we have with others and ourselves is considered psychologically profound, a useful map helping listeners and readers to contemplate our lives, draw on the experiences of others, and sensitize ourselves to emotions not always expressed in mundane daily discourse. But in the United States, ever since the mid-twentieth-century

McCarthy witch hunts,[1] poets and writers who examine the relationships between owners and owned or ask questions about class, race, and other areas of social conflict have been labeled "political." The term is most often meant to be pejorative. This is ominously like the sort of censorship that exists in severely authoritarian states, not those that proclaim themselves democratic.

In the U.S., to call a certain kind of poetry political has become a label, not a genre. It's an accusation that limits and derides. It is dismissive, just as it is dismissive to refer to poets as regional or local, implying that they are worthy of the title in their locality but not on a larger stage. "Political poet" is an epithet meant to denote a hack whose work is propaganda at worst, at best writing concerned with ideas that are somehow inferior to those that belong in poetry, a form that they claim should be above such mundane considerations.

There are people who use the label "political poet" in a neutral way or may even mean it as a compliment. What they don't realize is that all such definitions circumscribe and limit. Despite the existence of centuries of exquisite love poetry in all languages, when we note that so-and-so writes love poems, we most often mean that they produce the saccharine verse that appears on Hallmark greeting

---

1. During the Cold War aftermath of World War II, Senator Joseph McCarthy (1908–1957) claimed Soviet and Communist spies had infiltrated U.S. political institutions, universities, the film industry, and other areas of intellectual life. He held hearings at which he subpoenaed and questioned those accused. Some denounced their colleagues; others would not speak. Many lost their jobs or were imprisoned. Some committed suicide. Among the many byproducts of this period was the sense that a progressive point of view was an impediment to getting ahead. The chill on American letters lasted many years after McCarthy himself was discredited. Its pall continues in some academic circles today.

cards. When we say someone is a pastoral or landscape poet, we are saying that their work is passive and low-key, devoid of the highs and lows that sound when writing about other subjects; we do not imagine them conveying the drama of monumental weather events or the effect global warming is having on our planet. In a society in which politics has been reduced to the crass power struggles among those who twist language and deed to personal benefit, we stigmatize someone when we call them a political poet.

I write about everything that touches me: my New Mexico high desert landscape; the realities of being a woman, feminist, lesbian, mother, grandmother, and great-grandmother at the beginning of the twenty-first century; memory, its erasure and enduring pull; shame, crisis, injustice, fear, death, and everyday experience. Within that broad and diverse sweep, politics demands attention. Not the narrow partisan politics that characterizes both ends of the spectrum ("both sides of the aisle," as the pundits are so fond of saying), but the deeply political themes we invariably inherit and that bear on the ways we choose to live our lives. My poems have more questions than answers. I explore the connective tissue to be found beneath the camouflage of everyday events. Because nothing is foreign to my pen, political issues included, I am frequently called a "political poet."

I reject the label.

My life journey took me from my birth in the year of Spain's Civil War (often referred to as "the last good war"), childhood in a white upper-middle-class suburb of New York City, west to New Mexico with my parents and siblings in the 1940s, adolescence in provincial America during the stultifying 1950s, back to New York at the end of that decade where I lived among the city's abstract expressionist painters and Beat poets, then on to Mexico during the turbulent 1960s, revolutionary Cuba during the 1970s, Nicaragua where a new people's revolution was taking its first steps during the 1980s, and finally a return to my homeland where I was forced to fight a deportation order by the U.S. government because it considered some of my books to be "against the good order and happiness of the United States."[2]

How would it have been possible for me to write accurately and convincingly of my time and the places in which I've lived without including political observation in my work? And yet I was also soaking up cultures, languages, peoples, customs, and landscapes. And I continued to love, mother, marvel at nature, and follow many other passions. All of these elements found their way into my poetry and, in fact, it is precisely where they intersect that I often find what I want to say.

In early 2020, the world was seized by a plague, a highly infectious influenza-like illness that sickened people and killed them worldwide across all economic, social, and political lines. The first COVID-19 case was said to have been in Wuhan, China: a perfect pretext for racist fingerpointing. Needless to say, the poorest and most vulnerable members of society everywhere suffered measurably more than the wealthy and others protected by privilege. Aid was apportioned unevenly and inadequately. This was a public health crisis but also a highly political scenario. Statistics were tabulated daily but told a partial story. They showed a picture weighted by inequality and generated a chaos of fear while unable to convey the ways in which the

---

2. In 1967, while married to a Mexican, I'd acquired Mexican citizenship. When I returned to the U.S. in 1984, the government invoked the 1952 McCarran-Walter Immigration and Nationality Act to order me deported because of opinions expressed in some of my books. My case lasted five years, and I won it in 1989. This is an actual quote from one of the decisions rendered against me.

pandemic was affecting the world as we have known it. The differences between how the crisis was being addressed by nations that care for their citizens and those with neofascist regimes demonstrated this inequality in starkly brutal terms. Everything seemed political. In truth, everything was political, and also deeply human.

I found myself writing poems out of and about the pandemic. These poems emerged in a sustained surge of creativity. Sometimes I wrote two or three or more in a single day. I began posting them on Facebook. People responded. It was clear that I was asking the questions others were asking, searching for answers and finding only wish lists. Expressing shared fears and hopes. The world was changing around me. It still is. What kind of a world will we have when we have come through this devastation? Will we come through?

I soon realized that I had a book of poems. I called it *Starfish on a Beach: The Pandemic Poems*. Almost in tandem with my writing, a wonderful translator in Buenos Aires named Sandra Toro asked if she could render the work in Spanish. In July, a bilingual edition—*Starfish on a Beach: The Pandemic Poems / Estrellas de mar sobre una playa: los poemas de la pandemia*—appeared from Abisinia Editorial in Argentina and Editorial Escarabajo in Colombia. In October, Wings Press published an English-only edition in the United States. A couple of Chinese students in Minneapolis translated several poems into Mandarin. Requests for interviews about my process writing this collection continue to come in. Magazines on three continents continue to ask permission to publish selections from it.

This body of work certainly mirrors the politics of the pandemic, and also the fear it engendered, the small acts of kindness between individuals, and the cruel acts of abandonment on the part of the powerful forces at play. Risk opens us to what may come next. Social prejudices, cultural tendencies, and unexpected outcomes all show up in this book. Are these political poems written by a political poet? Or are they, like all the poems I write, reflections of life as we know it at a particular moment in time: bearing witness, giving free rein to vision, and making room for imagination?

How do words that have always had neutral meanings acquire negative ones in the public consciousness? We have seen this happen repeatedly. Communism was one of a number of ways of organizing society, like socialism or capitalism. Since the victory of the Russian Revolution and the Soviet state, McCarthy and those like him succeeded in getting us to think of it stereotypically; it became a catchall for a rigid authoritarian government that wanted nothing more than to destroy the American way of life. And this popular connotation persisted long after the fall of the Soviet Union and the dilution of international communism. The word *liberal* suffered a similar distortion, and neoliberalism was heralded as a positive policy when in practice it has meant domination and exploitation for millions. Similarly, globalization has been touted as a coming together of peoples when it has a generated a greater-than-ever breach between the very rich and miserably poor.

The word *ideological* has been twisted to mean leftist people or ideas, when its original meaning relates to any system of ideas from right or left. The same can be said of the word *political*. When those on the right accuse us of being "too political," they are saying that we are too far left, when in fact to be political is simply to understand the world in political terms. When those of us who write poetry are called "political poets," we are being told that our poems reflect a leftist point of view. In truth, every expression puts forth a point of view of one stripe or another. Discourse that avoids taking a stand assumes a default position which is likely to be conservative.

During the Trump presidency, words and their meanings were twisted as never before. *Antifa*, for example, which stands for antifascist, became an epithet. The term *cancel culture* is still being applied to the movement to tear down the monuments to racist leaders and remove offensive names from sports teams. The idea of cancel culture implies that those of us effecting change are erasing our culture or history rather than providing a much-needed corrective to the plethora of offensive statues that desecrate our landscape. As someone who believes in women's equality—a longtime and proud feminist—I know all too well how the word *feminist* has been degraded until a whole generation of women who believed in equality refused to identify as feminists. By sheer force of repetition, lies are accepted as truths. It is too bad that we haven't been able to retrieve the word *political*, restoring it to its rightful meaning.

If we cannot reclaim the political as a natural part of life, let us at least condemn and reject the condescension with which the term is wielded, as perhaps Shakespeare himself would have.

The Dictator

AS A CHILD, he may have desperately wanted to please his cold and distant father. His mother may have tried to treat him with love and teach him to be more empathetic but had her hands full dealing with how her husband treated her. Perhaps the boy saw how his father, a successful businessman, was revered in the community. Maybe he was bullied at school and learned that being the bigger bully kept his tormentors at bay. Weakness was clearly a disadvantage, weakness or the appearance of weakness. His male models were all sexist, racist, domineering, and in control: qualities highly valued in the men he knew.

Or perhaps none of this was true. The future dictator may have had a perfectly happy childhood. Maybe no parental treatment would have pushed him in one direction or another. Maybe he carried the sickness in his genes. Patriarchy creates the perfect petri dish for such behavior, and decent men must fight against it just as we must all fight against the fear of the Other we are taught from birth.

Whatever the case, aggressive self-interest must have gotten the future dictator what he wanted. Clearly it was his ticket to power, and power made him feel good. Nothing else made him feel so good.

As he grew, his social success and appearance of success told him he was on the right track. Lies and coverups paved his way to kingpin status. He married the most beautiful and compliant woman who would have him and, when she aged, traded her in for a younger, prettier model. He bought each new wife the biggest diamonds, the most expensive and ostentatious fur coats. And he had his pick of women on the side. He believed he was entitled to them all. He took it for granted they were delighted with his advances. The future dictator taught all his children, especially his sons, to be as much like him as possible; they too would have their pick of glamorous women.

When he failed at a business venture, he lied and exaggerated its profitability. He consistently blamed others for his mistakes. And he managed to build an empire of fake successes, as glittering as they were precarious.

Then the future dictator decided he wanted more power, enough to own a country, or perhaps the world. He ran for the highest office in the land. No one, including him, thought he could win. He was too unorthodox, too crude. But by now he was a master at manipulating people's fears and validating their basest instincts. Racism. Classism. Sexism. Homophobia. Xenophobia. Scorn for the most vulnerable. Language that people wanted to hear, to mimic, to use to validate their own uncomfortable feelings. At rally after rally, "Make America Great Again" became the mantra the man's followers repeated, louder and then louder still.

The future dictator also played with people's more legitimate longings, their feelings of inferiority and insecurity in the face of an arrogant discourse on the part of those then in public office. He painted himself as Everyman, frustrated with politics-as-usual and ready to bring transparency to the presidency. "Drain the swamp," he cried, while settling ever more comfortably into the swamp himself. And all the while he honed his own deviousness and dishonesty, made behind-the-scenes deals, took arch-criminals as partners, and made absolute loyalty his foremost demand.

Much to everyone's surprise, the future dictator won the election. His win was suspect but billed as a mandate. A sociopath became president of the United States. He did so by using every trick in his arsenal. When challenged about this or that, he simply lied. By virtue of their repetitions, his lies became truth. Now that he was president, his power increased. He surrounded himself with people who would follow his orders without question or argument. When his advisers challenged him, he replaced them with others. His staff broke records for turnover.

The dictator treated colleagues and nations with equal disdain. He gravitated toward the world's other dictators, calling them "my friends" and "very nice people." Few questioned these characterizations with any result. The dictator wrote new law, favoring profit and the destruction of resources, the erasure of public safety measures, the degradation of women and minorities.

Few in his political party dared oppose him. Few in the opposition party had the power to stand up to him in any effective way. Attempts to rein in the dictator's power played like bad theater with no end of season in sight. The press, battered by the dictator's ire and scorn, informed on these theatrical events as if their conclusions were not preordained. Every time it did so, it gave the dictator free publicity. The dictator emerged from each attempt to rein him in with renewed confidence, bravado, and, yes, support.

But wait. The dictator didn't possess real self-confidence. He may have been the least secure person ever to rise to such high office. No matter. An appearance of confidence was enough.

Except for other dictators, the world's leaders began making plans to work around the United States and forge alliances with more reasonable governments. After the dictator withdrew the country from major international treaties and refused to pay its fair share of monetary contributions to international agencies, these plans were consolidated. Inside the country, the political opposition proved incapable of uniting behind a candidate that could best the dictator. It didn't really matter, because the dictator had engineered a variety of ways of winning a second term. He would do so legally, illegally, or simply by claiming victory.

Every other national center of power was afraid of the dictator, from the Armed Forces to the Justice Department, from major corporations to the unions. The dictator had succeeded in replacing cabinet members and department heads with puppets loyal to his whims. He'd appointed enough federal judges so that the justice system could be counted on to favor injustice. And he'd vastly increased the profit margin for corporations, making the rich richer and further disempowering the poor.

The dictator had damaged education and healthcare beyond recognition. National parks were abandoned, some due to damage from nearby fracking, others because there was no money to run them. Funding for the arts was slashed to a minimum; museums and concert halls required private financial backing to stay open, and many closed. Neighborhoods and schools grew more segregated, prisons privatized and overflowing with people of color, homelessness to an all-time high. When the devastating COVID-19 pandemic surged, the dictator and his henchmen took advantage of the situation to promote policies they'd not been able to implement before.

Soon, one-third of U.S. cities lacked potable drinking water. Women lost control over our bodies; we could no longer get abortions or even reproductive healthcare in most states. High school graduates had little chance of going on to college, and children were left paying for decades of their parents' educational loans. Toxic waste sites invaded poor neighborhoods. It was no longer possible to survive a summer without powerful air conditioning units; if they broke down, people died. Everyone was kept busy trying to pick up the pieces.

The dictator declared himself president for life. He destroyed decades of mutually beneficial treaties with other nations; sealed the fate of climate change; maligned, imprisoned, and tortured every adversary; and finished installing sold-out judges in lifetime positions of power. The collective post-traumatic stress he imposed upon the nation affected people generations into the future. Any voice raised against him automatically became an attack that only made him more vindictive. His punishment for disobedience was swift and total.

Still, no one called the dictator a dictator. They said he was sick, narcissistic, a liar, unfit for public office. Some went so far as to label him a sociopath. But a dictator, no. After all, we are a democracy. Our elections may be riddled with problems, but they are democratic.

No. Hitler was a dictator. Pol Pot was a dictator. Pinochet was a dictator. Pundits said it was important not to use exaggerated terminology. Criticism of his reign was erased from the history books. School texts referred to the dictator's rule as a period of authoritarianism, a negative parenthesis, a time when the economy performed well but civil liberties were threatened.

Presidents aren't called dictators in our democratic system, only in countries where a military coup has overthrown the government.

But this story didn't end as previous paragraphs suggest. Much against the dictator's will, he was voted out of office before he could claim a second term. But the danger remains for another such story to begin.

Alan Turing, or, the Fear of Difference

DURING WORLD WAR II, Britain and other European nations engaged in desperate resistance to the Nazi menace, including highly secret efforts to break Enigma. The German code specified upcoming attacks to the minute, including details of latitude and longitude. It was reset every night at midnight, automatically rendering each previous day's grueling work another failure.

British Intelligence hired cryptanalyst Alan Turing (1912-1954) onto the Bletchley Project to break this seemingly undecipherable code. Turing, a socially awkward but brilliant British mathematician and logician, is credited with being the father of artificial intelligence and the modern computer. While still at university, he wrote a paper titled "Computing Machinery and Intelligence." It opens with this sentence: "I propose to consider the question, 'Can machines think?'" This gives us some sense of his mind, even at a relatively young age.

He also succeeded in breaking the code.

Turing didn't work alone. He was part of a small group of thinkers—linguists, mathematicians, chess champions, crossword puzzle mavericks, and intelligence officers—who labored around the clock. Defying a variety of obstacles (not the least of these being that neither Britain's spymasters nor, at first, his colleagues at Bletchley could abide the man), the elite group worked tirelessly. They knew that their every failure meant a prolongation of the war.

Turing's socially awkward demeanor reflected a more complex picture. He may have fallen somewhere on what today we would call the autism spectrum: extremely literal in his perceptions of everyday conversation and social interaction, and unselfconscious about his brilliance. Because he refused to hide the fact that he believed himself smarter than they were, he tended to annoy his colleagues. And he didn't suffer fools easily.

Turing was also a homosexual at a time when it was against the law. Although he didn't seem to have been ashamed of that aspect of his identity, it gave his detractors ammunition for harassment and eventually outright attack. When confronted, he admitted his sexual identity, and the forces of law and order used his confession to destroy him. Turing spoke of his years at Bletchley as "a sexual desert," involved as he was in attempts to break the code. But because homosexuality was a crime in Britain at the time, and most people in power were homophobes, they went after Turing and eventually brought him up on charges of gross indecency. He was convicted, given a choice between two years in prison and chemical castration, and opted for the latter. The hormone treatments destroyed his health—both physically and mentally—and he committed suicide a year later.

Many years later it was suggested that the Apple logo may be a secret tribute to Turing, with the bite mark a reference to his death (he committed suicide, some say, by eating a cyanide-laced apple). Asked if this was in fact the logo's origin, Apple founder and CEO Steve Jobs responded: "God, we wish it were."

It wasn't until 2013 that the British government, overcome by a petition with thirty thousand signatures, issued a posthumous pardon and, following in the footsteps of scientific communities that had already honored Turing everywhere, officially recognized his great contribution to the war effort, as well as to the field of artificial intelligence.

Turing's story, pivotal in breaking the Nazi hold on Europe, was personally tragic and socially representative. I find myself extrapolating from Turing's discovery to what technology does today, and from his painful life to the ways in which so many people who have extraordinary things to offer are held back and ostracized because of who they are. In Turing's case, the British government needed him desperately enough that they let him do his work until he helped them win the war. Then he became disposable.

Difference so often provides an excuse to marginalize, taunt, and even destroy those who give us our greatest scientific breakthroughs, philosophical revelations, and works of artistic genius. Jealousy and fear turn to hate. No society has been immune to this thoughtless cruelty. Today's propensity for bullying at ever-younger ages robs us of too many future geniuses—or simply well-adjusted happy human beings. And it often seems that moments of great intellectual flowering are prone to the sort of corrupt power plays that result in sidelining those whose vulnerability and genius make them targets of our ignorance and fear.

Socrates comes to mind. Giordano Bruno. Joan of Arc. Spinoza. And in more recent times, Allen Ginsberg, Daniel Ellsberg, Adrienne Rich, Temple Grandin, Edward Snowden, Chelsea Manning, and Caster Semenya. Being queer, female, Jewish, Communist, Black, or autistic, not fitting into a "normal" identity, or simply allowing brilliance and courage to challenge the status quo: these differences produce in us a socially conditioned fear, repulsion, sense of superiority, or opportunity to build ourselves up by putting others down.

Tragically, rather than reveling in the collective empowerment of difference, we attempt to calm our own fears by destroying those whose ideas or talents challenge what we have been taught is socially acceptable. Where would humanity be today without the Socratic method, Bruno's ability to see past religious ignorance, or the belief that citizens deserve to know what governments are doing in their names? How may we absolve ourselves of the shame of having put a great athlete such as Semenya through the humiliation of gender testing?

A particularly egregious case of such bigotry is the scientific community's treatment of Rosalind Franklin (1920–1958). Franklin was an English chemist and X-ray crystallographer who made critical contributions to the understanding of the fine molecular structures of DNA. Working in laboratories where women were few and had to struggle to have their work taken seriously, she produced the first image leading to the confirmation of DNA's double helix: the proof without which all future work in the area would have been impossible.

James Watson (b. 1928) and Francis Crick (1916–2004) saw her images. And in 1962, four years after Franklin's breakthrough, it was Watson and Crick who won the Nobel Prize in Physiology or Medicine "for their discoveries concerning the molecular structure of nucleic acids and its significance for information transfer in living material," sharing it with another male colleague, Maurice Wilkins. No mention of Franklin's contribution was made, either at the award ceremony itself, in the winners' other statements at the time, or in their reminiscences for years thereafter. Rosalind Franklin died of ovarian cancer at the age of thirty-seven. Her cancer may have been caused by her laboratory experiments involving radiation.

It is immeasurably sad to me that we have hidden so long behind our cruelty to those we are able to mock as different. Class, gender, racial, or sexual difference is still so often an acceptable excuse for social segregation, cruel jokes, or denial of opportunity, extending even to imprisonment, torture, and murder.

Thinking about Alan Turing—his significant contribution to defeating fascism as well as his terrible loneliness, forced "choice" of chemical castration, and suicide—make me question my own fears of difference. I ask myself if I can always say that I am courageous enough to denounce the hurtful joke, challenge bigotry, and embrace my fellow humans when and where it matters most.

Breaking the Maya Code: Creativity across Continents and Time

IN NOVEMBER 2013, BARBARA AND I TRAVELED through El Salvador, Honduras, Guatemala, Belize, and Mexico, following one of the many Maya Routes. (Ancient Maya sites exist throughout all these countries, with new sites being discovered all the time.)

I have visited Maya sites throughout Central America and southern Mexico over a period of many years: Palenque in Chiapas; Chichén-Itzá, Uxmal, Cobá, the smaller sites of the Ruta Puuc, and Tulúm in the Yucatán and Quintana Roo; Lamanai in Belize; El Tajín, Xochicalco, and the vibrant frescoes at Cacaxtla; Tikal, Quiriguá, and Yaxhá in Guatemala; the Asiatic-looking faces on the stela at Copán, Honduras. And I have not even scratched the surface. Even as I write, today's news brings a report of another recently discovered site in the rainforest of eastern Mexico. It is called Chactún, and forty thousand people may have lived there from 600 to 900 CE. These days, such sites are unearthed several times a year.

On that 2013 trip, I added an earlier and more primitive site to my list: Joya de Cerén in El Salvador. Rather than the monumental stone of the better-known sites, this one was constructed of adobe. A succession of volcanic explosions caused Joya de Cerén's abandonment, but layers of earth and lava teach us about how people lived there.

I have long been fascinated by the sites of ancient communities throughout the world. But the Maya evoke in me a special sense of connection. I have read everything I have been able to get my hands on about those extraordinary people. Eight million of them, inheritors of a magnificent legacy, continue to live in the villages, towns, and cities that dot southern Mexico and Central America.

The origins of the Maya are still shrouded in mystery. Some scholars believe their ancestors traveled south from Siberia across the Bering Strait land bridge some fourteen thousand years ago. Others point to evidence of Mesoamerican settlements as early as 18,000 BCE. Radiocarbon dating has identified groups of hunter-gatherers around eleven thousand years before our era. One of the earliest known artifacts from Maya country is a small projectile point of obsidian found by a picnicking schoolboy at San Rafael in the hills just west of Guatemala City. It is very similar to the Clovis point. An earlier generation of Maya scholars, particularly Sylvanus G. Morley, believed the Maya were the first to domesticate corn. And the proto-Mayan language (there are thirty Mayan languages today) was spoken before 2000 BCE, well within the Archaic Period.

Maya innovation and resistance survived the Spanish Conquest (often described as the most devastating holocaust in history; 90% of the native population was murdered) and still face ongoing cultural devastation, policies of extermination, impoverishment, and racism aimed at indigenous peoples. As architects, the Maya are unsurpassed. One has only to consider the monumental pyramids of Tikal, rising hundreds of feet above the jungle growth. And those marvels were constructed without any of today's building machinery or engineering tools. Maya statuary, ceramics, and jewelry display a genius in design as well as in their use of diverse materials. The codices, great illuminated books hand-written and painted on accordion-like parchment pages, hold their own beside the great books of other cultures. Tragically, the Spanish burned as many of these codices as they could find. Only five remain, coming to us in partial or damaged states. The Maya are credited with having invented the concept of zero, and their calendars are exemplary. They also produced the first processed chocolate.

As for classic Maya literature, the *Popol Vuh* rivals the Christian Bible or any other sacred book in terms of its origin narrative and literary beauty. In its creation story, the gods fashion humans first from mud, then from wood, and then from flesh—but all fail to thrive. Then the gods turn to maize, or corn, as the material capable of producing viable humans. These are their ancestors; they are the People of Corn.

Early on, the Maya discovered that by adding white lime and water to ground corn they could make *nixtamal*, which continues to be the basis for tortillas throughout modern-day Mesoamerica. Nixtamal's importance can't be overemphasized. Maize is naturally deficient in essential amino acids and niacin. A population whose diet consisted solely of untreated corn would have developed pellagra and could not have survived. Cooking the corn with lime enhances the balance of essential amino acids and frees the otherwise inaccessible niacin. Without the invention of this complex technique, no settled life in Mesoamerica would have been possible. Sadly, for these People of Corn, modern genetic modification of the plant is now playing havoc with their health and traditions and dangerously disrupting their lives.

Another interesting piece of Maya dynastic history is the fact that the long lines of rulers, honored in hieroglyphic tableaus at many of the ancient cities, include a number of women. These genealogies emphasize wars and conquest, and male leaders are in the majority. But names such as Lady Jaguar Shark, Lady Yohl Ik'nal, and Lady Six Sky are scattered among them, piquing my curiosity as to who they were and how they governed. Did they do so differently from the men?

Decades of state violence in Guatemala have uprooted the modern-day Maya from their traditional lands and decimated their numbers. In Mexico and Honduras, criminal gangs and drug cartels have brought uncertainty into their villages. Yet they remain.

And the Maya continue to preserve their traditions, passing them on from one generation to the next. Centuries ago, the Spanish Church burned their books and prohibited their intricate writing, yet in recent phases of scholarly decipherment Maya scribes have been able to help reimagine the meaning of many hieroglyphs.

Often prevented from acquiring an education because of marginalization and poverty, many of today's Maya have nonetheless struggled to reinsert themselves into the arena of scholarship pertinent to their own and world history. Rigoberta Menchú, a Maya woman from the highlands of Guatemala, was awarded the Nobel Prize for Peace in 1992. Her personal story, told in the book *I, Rigoberta Menchú*, put a human face on Guatemala's thirty years of extreme institutional violence, in which forty thousand people were uprooted, tortured, murdered, and disappeared.

Knowledge about the Maya has revealed itself slowly, and not without contradictions and setbacks. As a poet, I am fascinated with the still-unfolding history of deciphering Maya writing. This has often been referred to as "breaking the Maya code." The endeavor has spanned centuries and continents, and breakthroughs have come from scholars of many disciplines, artists, adventurers, and even children. Astonishingly, two Russians—Yuri Valentinovich Knorozov (1922-1999) and Tatiana Proskouriakoff (1909-1985)—contributed in fundamental ways to an eventual breakthrough, despite being greatly limited by the Soviet era's repressive insularity.

Theirs is a story worth repeating for what it teaches us about the pomposity of preconceived ideas, a paternalistic disregard for the achievements of peoples outside the discipline or considered "primitive," the disdain of anti-communist prejudice, and eminences who may in fact turn out to have been emperors without clothes.

For many years, British anthropologist Sir Eric Thompson (1898-1975) was considered the authority among those studying Maya writing. He had no university degree, nor did he hold a post at any institution of higher learning. But for a year he read in anthropology at Cambridge and came to dominate modern Maya studies through the sheer force of his personality. In 1926, he accepted a position at Chicago's Field Museum of Natural History, and from there he influenced generations of Maya scholars. Thompson eventually concentrated on deciphering non-calendric Maya symbols. The story of his ideas and interaction with other Maya scholars is long and complex. Some of his ideas were real contributions. But his own shortcomings—both academic and ideological—prevented him from seeing the forest for the trees.

The first real breakthrough in deciphering the Maya code came from the least likely of places. The Soviet Union, under Stalin, was a scene of intellectual repression; those who went against the dictator's ideas could find themselves banished to the gulag or worse. Scholarly innovation, except that which directly contributed to national development, was almost impossible. Yet it was in these restrictive circumstances, in 1952, that Yuri Valentinovich Knorozov, a thirty-year-old investigator at Leningrad's Institute of Ethnology, published an article called "Ancient Writing of Central America."

In the Marxist state, Knorozov had received an excellent undergraduate and graduate education. He studied many different forms of writing, including Sumerian, Chinese, Japanese, and Arabic. His professors urged him to concentrate on Egyptology. But his interests were more wide-ranging, and also comparative. (The latter is what eventually enabled him to challenge Thompson's assumptions.)

In 1947, Knorozov's teacher, Sergei Aleksandrovich Tokarev, posed a question to his pupil: "If you believe that any writing system produced by humans can be read by humans, why don't you try to crack the Maya system?" Knorozov set about to learn Spanish and devoted the rest of his life to doing what his mentor had suggested. His accomplishment is all the more extraordinary if we consider that not until he was an old man, when Gorbachev finally loosened travel restrictions, was he able to travel to Central America, contemplate the great cities of Palenque and Tikal, and gaze upon an authentic Maya inscription. Before then, his knowledge of the field had come exclusively from photographs.

At the time, the academic establishment accepted Thompson's ideas, which emanated from a paternalistic and Eurocentric inability to assign the people who made the glyphs the intellectual complexity required to have created anything but random images. A few scholars, however, among them Michael Coe (1929–2019), long regarded as the supreme historiographer of Maya studies, read Knorozov's article and were excited by it. The Russian accepted the prevailing notion that the glyphs represented sounds, or syllables. But, based on his broad knowledge of scripts from other parts of the world, he also knew that the signs could have more than one function. He understood they might sometimes be inverted for calligraphic purposes, and that phonetic signs might be added to morphemic ones to lessen ambiguity in the reading. Knorozov compared some of the texts in the codices with the pictures that accompanied them. In what turned out to be a groundbreaking article, he concluded: "the system of Maya writing is typically hieroglyphic and in its principles of writing does not differ from known hieroglyphic systems."

Thompson spent most of the rest of his life trying to discredit Knorozov. Cold War ideological bias bolstered his dismissiveness. But the great barrier to deciphering the Maya glyphs had been shattered. Fresh minds from a variety of disciplines, no longer constrained by Thompson's authority, contributed bits and pieces to the puzzle.

Another Russian, Tatiana Proskouriakoff, came to the United States with her family in 1915, and thus did not have to face the ideological limitations, lack of technology, or restriction on travel suffered by Knorozov. She graduated from a U.S. university in 1930 with a degree in architecture and ended up on a number of archaeological expeditions to Central America, producing thousands of drawings of pyramid elevations and the glyphs that adorn them. Her great contribution was charting in accurate detail the dynastic records at Piedras Negras in Guatemala's Petén region. This work, too, was central to the decipherment.

Dozens of more recent archaeologists, anthropologists, linguists, and other specialists followed these early scholars, all of whom contributed in one way or another to breaking the Maya code. Sylvanus Morley was a bridge to more contemporary minds such as Coe, David Kelley, Floyd Lounsbury, Linda Schele, and George and David Stuart, among others.

Stuart's story fascinates me. At the age of three, he was taken on his first trip to the archaeological wonders of Mexico and Guatemala. His parents spent five months studying the city of Cobá, and he played among the ancestral sites, often with Maya children around his own age. On that trip he picked up a number of words in contemporary Yucatec Maya. As he got older and returned on others of his parents' field trips, he made drawings of the glyphs.

Back in Washington, D.C., in 1976, Stuart met Linda Schele. She was a consultant for a book called *The Mysterious Maya*, a project being undertaken by Stuart's parents for The National Geographic Society. At one point the eleven-year-old child, who had been sitting at a table where the adults were working, pointed to one of the pictures and announced: "That's a fire glyph." That evening, Schele invited the boy to spend several weeks with her the following summer at Palenque. She asked him to help her correct drawings of the important inscriptions at that site.

An unusual and extraordinarily positive aspect of contemporary Maya studies is that it has brought together people from many different disciplines—even some adventurers who do not call themselves scholars—and has held meetings at which old and young, professors and disciples, people in fields that ordinarily would not pay much attention to one another, all listen to and build upon each other's ideas. The academic jealousies so detrimental to true scholarship don't seem to be present at those meetings.

Linguists, totally disregarded in Thompson's time, played an important role in the decipherment which, during the 1980s, really began to take off. Since then, it has advanced at a dizzying pace. For those interested in this fascinating history, there is nothing better than *Breaking the Maya Code*, the feature documentary by David Lebrun. This two-hour film situates the decipherment within the context of our own history and culture in a way that allows us to follow it as if we ourselves were intimately involved. Through digital animation, we can trace the development and decipherment of a single glyph.

Many exciting discoveries on the long journey to decipher Maya writing poke at my poet's sensibility. One that is particularly interesting is that ancient Maya scribes didn't always draw a given glyph in the same way. They often let their imaginations and playfulness run wild. Glyphs have been found hiding behind or within other glyphs, an artistic abbreviation of the most creative sort. The drawing of glyphs also varied from region to region, language to language. Some eighty percent of Maya glyphs have now been deciphered, but learning the language is not the same as learning its cultural meaning or how it was spoken. For this, much work remains to be done. Such discovery will be achieved through a non-competitive sharing of information and a more complete understanding of the history and culture of the Maya people.

As a poet, I am fascinated by the differences between oral and written traditions, what part memory plays in language development, how the broader culture influences language and communication, the roles played by the conquest of one people by another, and many other variables. Why are some languages glottalized and others tonal? Why do some use complex rules of grammar while others seem almost grammar-free? At this point in the study of human history, it is more than clear that a people's cultural or philosophical complexity does not depend on the perceived complexity of its language.

I have never understood the distinction between prehistory and history, which is generally based on the existence of a written language. Images are a type of language to me, including the rock art found everywhere in the world, the Inca quipus, and certainly the glyphs developed by the Maya. Even the Rongorongo boards, found on Easter Island (Rapa Nui) and bearing lines of repeated symbols not associated with either letters or sounds, are communication of some kind. It is believed they once stimulated memory, enabling those who "read" them to refer to certain stories from the collective memory of their traditional past.

A great poem is a distillation of such communication.

How We Feed Ourselves

FROM THE REMOTE BEGINNINGS of human life on earth, scholars have traced our "progress" in all sorts of areas. I put the word *progress* in quotes because I want to talk about food. We have certainly progressed in many aspects of our lives, including our ability to prepare and preserve food, but there is disturbing evidence that we have not done so in terms of what we eat. The advent of agriculture probably changed our lives more than any other achievement. Just imagine what might happen if, instead of chasing profit, all of agribusiness from the largest conglomerate to the smallest family farm prioritized healthy growing, harvesting, and eating.

Although we have traveled a long way from our hunter/gatherer ancestors, who foraged for and trapped what they could find to satisfy their hunger, in important ways we eat less healthfully today. We eat out of season. And genetic seed modification and cross-pollination, over-processing, colorants, pesticides, and the chemical additives that fill our fast foods contaminate and strip away the nutrients we need.

Over time, vitamins and minerals have been bred out of many foods. Longer shelf life and attractive packaging have taken their place. It is much more important to corporate America's bottom line that a food product survive long-distance shipping than that we eat what is good for us.

Obesity is now one of the most insidious killers of people in the United States. Almost three million people die each year because they are overweight, and the prevalence of obesity nearly tripled between 1975 and 2016. The American Medical Association has listed the condition as a disease, deserving of the research funding allotted to other ills such as cancer. And the offshoots of obesity—diabetes, high blood pressure, heart conditions, and the like—kill hundreds of thousands of people each year and cost our broken healthcare system millions in unnecessary expense.

Yet for the dearth of health in what we ingest, we enjoy an astonishing variety of food cultures. We may be fortunate enough to visit Bangkok, Thailand, where tiny coconut-filled buns melt in our mouths. We may have been to Puebla, Mexico, where the best *mole* (a rich brown sauce that combines peanuts, sesame seeds, chocolate, and seventeen different types of chile) is made. If we aren't that fortunate, our experience of Thai—or Mexican, Indian, French, Italian, Chinese, Japanese, Peruvian, and dozens of other global cuisines—may be limited to a local restaurant. Whichever the case, the tastes of foreign foods (and regional dishes in our own country) go a long way toward helping us understand and appreciate other cultures.

So much of how we contemplate life and live it in the everyday resides in the foods we eat and how we prepare them. I can't forget working in the high Andes of Peru, where people share meals from a common dish; or the satisfying breakfasts of sticky rice wrapped in banana leaves I enjoyed in North Vietnam during my 1974 fieldwork there.

A more complicated memory involves taking a group of U.S. American women to a rabbit farm in Cuba. This was during the difficult 1990s, when that country was suffering from severe economic stress. The rabbits lived in spotless waist-level coops where their droppings fell through a grid and fed a worm farm below. The worms, in turn, enriched soil for crops. On the day of our visit the farmworkers, most of them women, had been up before dawn cutting tomatoes and cucumbers into beautiful shapes that simulated flowers and preparing other aspects of an astonishing feast. Nothing was wasted at this cooperative. But the rabbits were rabbits, cute little bunnies, and several women in the group refused to eat them. It was hard explaining their reluctance to our bewildered hosts.

Modern farm subsidies, misleading labeling, poor meat slaughtering and processing practices, agribusiness, and political manipulation of food imports skew the ways in which we relate to food. Mexican novelist Laura Esquivel may have said more than she intended when she wrote: "If we return to the cosmic, we Mexicans are children of maize, and people in the United States have eaten enough popcorn by now to be counted as kin." Esquivel was making a wry observation about cross-border familiarity and friendship. I read her words as symbolic of the U.S. penchant for taking real food and turning it into something quick, jazzy, and of limited nutritional content.

Indeed, communities throughout the world claim to be children of maize, or corn. Here in the Southwest, we thrill to the sight of a pile of corncobs chewed clean by our Ancestral Puebloan forebears eight hundred years ago. Many Native American tribes today believe they were born of the Corn Mother. The corn stalk, with its beautiful green leaves, silken tassels, and healthy ears, is a symbol of fertility to many. But in recent years, Monsanto and other U.S.-based multinational corporations have decimated the diversity of corn reproduction. By genetically modifying the plant, these scientific Svengalis, aided by the wind that carries the altered seed everywhere, have made sure that only their seeds and their pesticides can be used for generations into the future. In India, over the past several decades, hundreds of farmers have committed suicide because they have lost a tradition of planting and harvesting that has been their legacy for all remembered time.

Corn has also played a part in the erasure of vitamin content. The real nutrients reside in the old multicolored Indian corn, now sold almost exclusively as a table decoration. As a commercially conditioned public demands sweeter corn, the ears have been bred whiter and whiter—substituting sugar for those properties that for thousands of years sustained people for whom corn was the main staple. Corn syrup is also now added to almost everything, increasing our sugar intake.

Food in the United States is no longer primarily nourishing, wisely medicinal, or even creative in the majority of cases. It has become temptation, addiction, ostentation, and corporate manipulation. In only a minority of our public schools have lunches been improved to include fruits and vegetables and minimize fats and sugars. Most schools still have soda machines lining their halls, from which young people consume the popular soda pops and other soft drinks that decay their teeth and increase their chances of suffering early onset diabetes. When a New York City mayor proposed downsizing soft drinks sold in the city, the uproar was immediate; many perceived him as impinging upon their individual rights. We may remember President Reagan's claim that ketchup is a vegetable. Such rationalization has only gotten worse.

Fast food loaded with sugar and fat is the staple of the American diet, especially for the growing population groups that must resort to McDonald's and similar chains to feed their families. A Big Mac meal—which comes with a Big Mac burger, a medium order of French fries, and a medium soft drink—contains 1,100 calories, forty-four grams of fat, 149 grams of carbs, 1,225 milligrams of sodium, and only twenty-nine grams of protein. Add ketchup, and the calorie count goes up. But this meal costs less than one sweet bell pepper at a gourmet market. Those who urge a mother on food stamps with a large family to feed to "buy healthy" have no idea how unrealistic the suggestion is.

We are playing with fire. I am intrigued by many of the new ways of eating: vegetarianism, veganism, raw food, paleo, farmer's markets, buying local, consuming smaller portions, and so forth. And I am among the fortunate. At this point, my income still allows me to make choices. Yet I am not immune to the occasional overly rich restaurant dish or super-sized dessert. The media message affects us all.

As a woman who raised four children and now enjoys ten grandchildren and two great-grandchildren, and as a longtime feminist, I am also more than a little interested in women's relationship to food. A mother's experience feeding her family. What a grandmother or great-grandmother observes as she watches younger family members eat. In 1995, I wrote a book of poems called *Hunger's Table: Women, Food & Politics*. It was published two years later by Papier Maché Press, a small house that soon after ceased to exist. The book was remaindered.

All the poems in *Hunger's Table* function as such, and simultaneously as recipes. During the book's brief run, I read from it in restaurant venues where enthusiastic cooks prepared some of the recipes for audiences always excited to share their own specialties or tell their personal food stories.

Food and women, women and food: it is a combination laced with joy, fraught with anxiety, and complicated by the ways in which patriarchy burdens women in every society.

In the introduction to *Hunger's Table* I wrote:

> The sometimes nurturing sometimes uneasy place we make for food in our lives, and the prohibitions and demands that enter us like poison-tipped arrows, shot from the patriarchal bowstring [often produce] unresolved conflict, more painful or contradiction-filled than we are able to articulate...
>
> How do we assimilate the bombardment of images: a skeletal child whose deadened eyes and pleading hands reach toward us from countries so distant to our experience... the Weightwatcher's silhouette, repeatedly straining against desire or even need... a commercial for stuffed-crust pizza followed by one for an exercise machine guaranteed to flatten that tummy or slim those thighs. Looking back to a time before written history, men are referred to as hunters, women as gatherers. The implication of such separateness continues to define who each of us learns to be. Yet there is something wrong with these assumptions. Food gathering in pre-agricultural times *was* hunting. Women's relationship to what nurtures successive generations remains misunderstood, off balance...
>
> In the Unites States, as recently as the turn of the [twentieth] century, food was synonymous with home for the vast majority of women. For Black women, that home frequently belonged to someone else, someone to whom they were linked by the most complex of exploitative relationships.

Working- as well as middle-class men might order a drink or two at their local saloon and partake of its free buffet. Workingwomen—many of them prostitutes—were also going to bars on both sides of the Atlantic. Soon their more aristocratic sisters began to have tearooms and a few restaurants where they could eat in the company of men, but none where they were welcomed with other women or alone.

Our foremothers shared their recipes with one another. Often written in a careful hand and passed from generation to generation, these histories are yet to be valued or even fully explored. Cooking and feeding are what we have always done. Poor women cook for others. The wealthy hire cooks. In most places today, men remain the highly respected and well-paid chefs at expensive restaurants, while we women cook for our families and for others—although what, how, and under what circumstances varies greatly from culture to culture.

The images are telling. A male restaurant chef appears immaculate in white, a traditional chef's hat increasing his height, his sensational irritability almost a requisite for fame. A woman is most often portrayed wiping her hands on a soiled apron as numerous small children pull at its hem. Yet she must struggle to be perfectly groomed and with dinner waiting when her husband returns from the world out there. In almost every language, the titles themselves describe dramatic difference: chef versus cook, temperament versus drudgery. Thus, gender intersects with class, race, and geographical location, further complicating a woman's relationship to food.

In the almost three decades since *Hunger's Table*, some of what I wrote no longer holds true. More and more women today demand a different relationship to the world, including those areas which involve food. A number of women are today recognized as brilliant chefs. The image of the perfectly groomed wife greeting her husband with dinner each night has faded in rapidly changing times. But anorexia, bulimia, and other eating disorders primarily target women. Gender continues to affect the way food plays out in our lives. We are still seduced by harmful diet products and deceptive get-thin-fast plans, and by a fashion industry that favors body types impossible to emulate.

Girl children still want Barbie, that icon of the impossible body measurements. The manipulation of food products continues to assault us, and women—who are overwhelmingly responsible for feeding our families— must contend with intentionally confusing labels, the mixed messages flooding us via the corporate media, and industries that increase their profits by pushing unhealthy and addictive foodstuffs. Our children continue to receive daily messages that make them want the fast food that will doom them to lifetimes of ill health.

Hunger's Table has poem-recipes that address the legacy of my own food culture and others, my mother's and my relationship as framed by food, a dish I once prepared for the woman who is now my wife and the three years it took her to admit she doesn't care for the dish or its preparation, and much else. I will close this essay with a poem that is a recipe for *baba ghannouj*, a Near Eastern blend of baked eggplant, tahini, parsley, garlic, and lemon, often served with wedges of pita bread:

Battered Woman Surprise

The great round purplish black eggplant
is quietly crazed in loneliness.
Not merely alone or needing space
but lonely in its full circumference.
Floating, burgundy, swollen in fear.

Prick her all over with the tines of a fork
then lay her directly on the rack
of an oven set to 400. In 45 minutes
she will shrink into herself, her polished skin
a defeated mass of wrinkles.

When cool enough to handle, scrape her flesh
to a bowl with ¼ cup sesame tahini,
lots of pressed garlic, finely chopped
parsley, salt, pepper, and the juice
from at least two lemons.

Now her blue-black sheen is gone, her fullness
barely remembered. But this delicacy
—chilled aphrodisiac—
may be scooped into a little center bowl
surrounded by Wheat Thins or melba toast.

Before serving, drizzle a bit of olive oil
across the top. Guests will enjoy
the exotic taste you share with them.
And the appetizer—improved for its own good—
will not complain.

Eating Out

A MORE ELEGANT PHRASE is *dining out*. Whatever the description, it refers to having a meal in a place that is not one's home. Sometimes the home of a friend, but more often one of the millions of public eateries, establishments where one pays to be cooked and served a repast of one's choice but not of one's making.

Steak house or vegetarian, vegan or seafood, soup and salad bars, five-star restaurants, cafeterias, old-style diners, food carts, a place where service matters and that ubiquitous thing called a tip is expected at the end. Or perhaps automation was the attraction; I'm thinking of New York's mid-past-century Automats where a nickel dropped in a slot sprang a small glass door behind which a sandwich, bowl of soup, or slice of pie waited. In the late 1950s, a friend's grandfather took us there, placing an equal number of nickels in each of our hands as he watched us make our choices. Even at the Automat, the vast majority of people couldn't afford to dine. Eating out has always been a luxury.

Restaurant history is shrouded in the complex stories of cultural demand, migration, and desire. The Roman Empire had them. Frozen in the ruins of Pompeii, evidence of 158 foodservice counters has been found; many locals may have been savoring their delicacies when the furious rush of hot ash stopped a spoon on its way to an open mouth.

Unaccompanied women were permitted only relatively recently to eat in public dining establishments. Until the mid-1800s, we were barred from restaurants where men held lunch meetings. Up until the 1960s, there were numerous bars in the United States where women were not allowed; in that decade, we launched the protests that eventually gave us access to places such as McSorley's Old Ale House on New York City's Lower East Side, and in 1970 that 116-year-old establishment was forced to admit us for the first time. Male-only clubs still exclude women. And racial segregation in the U.S. South disgraced restaurants, from the most elegant down to drug store soda fountain counters, until the 1964 passage of the Civil Rights Act made such exclusion unlawful.

In China, food catering establishments have been known since the eleventh century. They probably developed from the tea houses that catered to travelers across that vast land. The first Parisian cafe is said to have opened at the Saint-Germain fair in 1672, and fifty years later there were four thousand in the city. Eateries not connected with hotels didn't appear in the United States until the late eighteenth century, fairly recent as history goes. Here we make up in business innovation what we may lack in style, and franchises developed here—eventually bringing a McDonald's, Taco Bell, and International House of Pancakes to the streets of Ulan Bator or the Brazilian Amazon.

You won't find Mexican restaurants in Mexico or Chinese restaurants in China. As the poet said, smiling wryly at her audience: In Beijing they don't say "We're going to eat Chinese."[1] The novelty of a particular cuisine, or what passes itself off as such, can only exist where that cooking style is unique, exotic.

Immigrant communities support the best of their native foods transplanted far from home. Authentic ingredients may be hard to come by, and substitutes are developed. Generation to generation, a restaurant's menu may stretch to embrace the tastes of the host nation, giving birth to what we call modern fusion. At places where foods from other cultures are served, accommodation must be made for the foreigner's inability to ingest a fiery spice or local revulsion at what is considered a delicacy back home. I remember stopping along a highway in Thailand where women were ladling fried spiders from large vats of bubbling oil. Delicacy or playful challenge? For the tourist, probably both.

Most of us are shaped by the menus of our childhood homes, just as by the privation or abundance we knew there. My mother, who hated to cook but prided herself on a few iconic dishes, favored canned tuna and Velveeta cheese, sliced white bread and overcooked vegetables. Yet Dad loved taking the family out for a Sunday meal, and we often went to interesting places. Once seated around the table, he would invariably encourage us to "order whatever you want." We knew to be mindful of price, though, for if one of us asked for something at the high end, he would turn to our mother on the drive home and comment: "She just had to get the most expensive dish."

In seeming contradiction—my childhood home was filled with mixed messages, around food and everything else—Dad's expansive generosity came to the fore when he

---

1. Sawako Nakayasu made this remark at a poetry reading I attended at Naropa University in Boulder, Colorado, in the early 2000s.

took genuine delight in splurging. When I was fifteen, we visited New Orleans and he took us to Antoine's, at the time that city's best-known restaurant, founded in 1840. I remember we grabbed a cheap lunch at an Orange Julius—home of a strange concoction in a thick goblet that blended juice with milk and a raw egg—in order, he said, to be able to afford that evening's delight. Thinking back, I wonder if he really enjoyed eating at Antoine's or simply thought it was a glamorous thing to do.

In their old age, my parents went to Albuquerque's Furr's Cafeteria for lunch almost every day. I can still see them making their slow way through the familiar line, placing a chicken fried steak, small ration of vegetables, and piece of apple pie on their shared tray. They greeted the servers by name and clearly appreciated the comforting fare and friendly attention. By then their palates were tired of extravagance, in taste as well as cost.

My maternal grandfather, who sexually abused me when I was very young, also introduced me to Grand Central Station's oyster bar. Thinking about both circumstances curdles my stomach even today.

As I grew, like many women in our hypocritical society, I knew being thin was prized above all else. And like so many victims of such a value system, my elegantly diminutive mother urged me to watch my weight even while offering me a second dessert. It's a question of will, she always said. I struggled with fat for most of my life—until a time in my early eighties when my body decided to accommodate itself. There's no other way to describe it. One day I stopped eating more than I needed. Within a few months, I had lost forty pounds. I wasn't dieting. The weight loss wasn't intentional or desperate. It was as if my body had decided: if you can't do this, I guess I'll have to do it for you.

Eating Out

Yet I love to cook and bake. There's nothing like the scent of freshly baked bread filling the house.

My four pregnancies each brought out insatiable cravings for certain foods. With Gregory, I longed for a side order of creamed spinach at a German restaurant called Luchow's, not far from my 1950s New York City walkup. It was beyond my means, but that didn't deter me. I remember fingering the white linen tablecloth, pretending to peruse the menu, and then ordering two small servings and making them last as long as possible. The waitstaff came to regard me with bemused suspicion, but I kept on frequenting the place until days before giving birth. When pregnant with Sarah, I bought ripe avocados, cut them in half, removed the large seed, and filled the hollow with a particular brand of store-bought neon-orange salad dressing. Then I scooped out one spoonful after another, careful not to waste a bite. Awaiting Ximena and Ana, I longed for the tiny pork tacos that could be purchased only in one of the Aztec capital's all-night street stands; I can still see the broad knife slicing thin pieces of meat from a revolving spit onto miniature corn tortillas. I have read that food cravings during pregnancy indicate a vitamin or mineral deficiency. Really? Shaved pork speaks to me more about desire and deserved self-indulgence than it does about need.

Other restaurant moments emerge from memory. The day I left Mexico City, my home of the previous eight years, to exit the country illegally and make my way to Cuba via Czechoslovakia, my then-partner and I stopped for a meal at a Sanborn's, the popular chain combining pharmacy, upscale merchandise, and restaurant. The one we chose was the famous House of Tiles, in the city center. I had my favorite: *enchiladas suizas*. I've never eaten at a Sanborn's since—any Sanborn's—without remembering that dramatic day, when I wondered if I would ever see my beloved city again.

In Cuba, during the severe rationing of the 1970s, we were sometimes lucky enough to get a reservation for El Conejito, a restaurant near our apartment where every dish was a variation on rabbit. Rabbit stew. Braised rabbit. Rabbit spreads served with crackers. I would sit at the head of the table, a lady's boxy faux leather purse half-open in my lap. I had lined that purse with plastic and used it only for such occasions. When all family members had had their fill, they'd pass what remained on their plate down to me, and I'd shovel the leftovers into my purse. They sometimes lasted us for a week.

Restaurants are where the wealthy or simply those who can afford to eat out come in contact with some of the world's most poorly paid workers. Waitstaffs are increasingly composed of impoverished people of color, immigrants, and illegals who would be hard put to find another line of work. Often earning far below the minimum wage, they must depend on tips for a meager income.

When New York's World Trade Center was attacked on September 11, 2001, the Windows on the World restaurant, on the 106th and 107th floors of the North Tower, was the scene of overwhelming death as were all the doomed upper floors. But there was an important difference between the restaurant employees and those who worked at the brokerage houses and other offices in those buildings. The cooks and waitstaff at Windows on the World were mostly undocumented immigrants. Their families had to mourn them in silence and were unable to apply for the financial assistance offered to the families of the other victims.

The customer at an upscale restaurant, who may pay several hundred dollars for a meal, has nothing in common with the person who serves his table. Yet they need one another in this strange dance we call modern life.

Farewell to the Book?

A FEW YEARS BACK, a friend wrote to tell me her novella had been published. Where can I get a copy? Here's the link, she responded. When I went there, I discovered her book was only available on Kindle. No hardcopy at all. This was my first experience with what has since become commonplace: a gradual replacement of physical books with their digital imposters, something like cloning in a minor key.

Call me old-fashioned. I like to read real books, material objects with pages I can turn, a cover that draws me in, inked letters that in some cases even bear a faint whiff of the centuries-old bookmaking craft. I know it's the rare book today that was produced on a letterpress with anything resembling printer's ink. But the mass-produced facsimiles, especially when well designed, allow me to make believe.

Reading is, after all, often about make-believe. It transports us to distant lands, times before our own or in the future, people with whom we would not come in contact were it not for their stories preserved in print, ideas that agonize or delight us. Answers to questions we didn't know we had.

I know that the electronic versions of books—the Kindle, Apple Books, the Nook—deliver the same content. They even do so ever so much more expediently. Instead of lugging a heavy trunk, you can travel with several hundred titles inside a small handheld device. You can make the typeface larger or smaller, change the background from white with black letters to black with white letters or varying shades of gray, depending on your eyesight or light source. And by clicking on a word or phrase you can explore its history and meaning with dictionaries, thesauruses, and encyclopedias that enrich the experience.

But something doesn't feel right. It may be about the way form and content merge for me when the vehicle delivering them is what I expect. From ancient papyrus scrolls to contemporary paper pages bound in elegant cloth, the physical characteristics of books have traveled a rich history. Compare writing in the margins with making digital notes. Consider the touch of a cloth, leather, or even paper cover as opposed to the cold feel of a digital device. Imagine what their material essence said of papyrus scrolls, cuneiform engravings, glyphs etched into stone, or the codices of the Maya; surely their material form was as important as the content that can be read there. And we have a sumptuous tradition of artist books, one-of-a-kind objects with their own stories to tell. Curling up in the corner of a comfortable couch against a pile of cushions on a cold winter night almost demands a real book in hand. I understand all the advantages offered by the digital devices, but give me an old-fashioned tome.

Is it just that at my age I am not comfortable with progress? No. I traded my old film camera in for a digital model. I miss my darkroom but became proficient at

Photoshop when the time came. I use a cell phone and even got rid of my land line. The coronavirus pandemic pushed me to learn digital platforms in order to perform my work virtually. I do a great deal of research online and depend on email to connect me to the world.

This begs the question of digital periodicals. Why do I value them, when digital books disappoint? I think it must have to do with the fact that I expect a periodical to be constantly changing, of the moment, immediate and relevant to the here and now. Digitally delivered news media allow for community response, sometimes even blossoming into full-blown discussion.

But books are where I draw the line. I hope I do not live long enough to have to say farewell to books. Could it be because I am a writer and, although I appreciate my publishers making my words available on all the different platforms, I welcome each new physical book as if it were a newborn? From cover through interior format, I delight in what their designers do with the raw material I provide. I am always eager to see how they match their talents to mine, producing something elegant and inviting so that readers may delight in the experience. I've been fortunate in this respect: Bryce Milligan, the wonderful editor at Wings who designs and produces my poetry collections, has given me great gifts, particularly with a hand-bound limited edition of *As If the Empty Chair / Como si la silla vacía*, my suite of poems for Latin America's disappeared, and *Time's Language: Selected Poems 1959-2018*, chosen from thirty-one of my poetry collections. Duke University Press, where I have been publishing my nonfiction books, outdid itself with volumes such as *Only the Road / Solo el camino: Eight Decades of Cuban Poetry* and my memoir, *I Never Left Home: Poet, Feminist, Revolutionary*. For a companion volume, *My Life in 100 Objects*, I looked for a publisher I knew would be able to reproduce the hundred images in full color. I was thrilled when New

Village Press took the project on, and it, too, is a gorgeous object.

I have also been fortunate to have had many foreign editions of my work over the years, beautifully designed in Mexico, Ecuador, Argentina, Colombia, Brazil, Venezuela, Chile, Holland, Turkey, and Japan, among other countries. Different countries have different book-making traditions and styles. I love the book flap many of these editions use and that has all but gone out of style in the United States.

And because I love books, I love bookstores, especially the independent variety that enriched our communities before the chains did them in and now exist in vastly reduced numbers. I can spend hours in those wonderful places, staffed by people who know and love books. I never feel rushed or as if I were in some wholesale warehouse. I understand that those stores stock titles by publishers specializing in women's books, Latin American titles, and experimental literature. I know that the major publishers give preferential pricing to the chains, thereby influencing what a nation reads. Through this sort of collusion, our country's taste in reading is subtly but conclusively being shaped to reflect the needs of a corporate, consumerist, violent, and warmongering society. They would turn us into pawns in their system. Independent publishers and independent booksellers seem a last line of defense.

The invasion of the national chains went hand-in-hand with governmental defunding of libraries and schools cutting art and music so that students could spend all their time learning to take tests and spew names and dates from memory. Teaching to think has been replaced with rote memorization. The United States' world standing in innovation, creativity, and how well we educate our young has suffered as a result. And our "experts" still don't seem to grasp the reasons why.

As the past century waned, the city of Albuquerque, with fewer than than a million inhabitants, had The Living Batch, for decades one of the best literary bookstores in the country. It had Salt of the Earth, a marvelous general-interest store that also hosted years of important readings and lectures. We had Full Circle, one of the best-stocked women's bookstores, and then also Sisters and Brothers, a store featuring gay and lesbian literature. Trespassers William was the store where children could attend weekly storytelling sessions and find the perfect book for whatever age and taste. Each of these great stores eventually succumbed to the pressure of capitalist bookselling. Today we have only Bookworks, Page One, and Organic Books—too few in a city of our size to make up for those we've lost.

A few years after the demise of so many fine independent bookstores, Barnes & Noble and Borders—the chains that had done them in—had to face competition from Amazon.com, the mega online source for everything from books to appliances. The chains then too became victims of these changing times.

Amazon is a phenomenon with which it's hard to argue. I hate the corporate power it exerts over publishing and pricing, how authors and independent publishers are overlooked or exploited, and the sensationalist titles that it features. I hate watching a single powerful entity control how we acquire our food for thought. At the same time, I appreciate a single site where new and used editions can be found, where at least some of the savings are passed onto the buyer, and where readers can review and recommend books. I appreciate my own Amazon author's page, listing so many editions of my titles over the years.

In capitalism, progress too often means less attention is paid to issues of originality, craft, or the pride in making something beautiful. Mass production brings cost down and makes items more widely available, although most of what is saved goes into industry's pockets, leaving the consumer with little remedy or protection. Much more dangerous, and less discussed, is the fact that when corporations control production they also fabricate need—encouraging public interest in that which benefits big business. Getting a population to buy what will make it less able to think for itself and to be more dependent on what the corporate bosses are selling is an important part of the picture.

My attachment to the physical book may be a last gasp act of defiance, reminiscent of a different time, one in which independent thinkers could more easily start a small press and publish texts that would never have made it past the gatekeepers at Random House or Simon & Schuster. A time when I could call my independent bookseller and ask her to order a title that caught my fancy, or browse among bookshelves stocked with the unexpected, rebellious, and magical.

Yes, I think it is one woman's small statement: memory honored and unleashed. It is not about rejecting progress or failing to keep up with the times. I do all right in those areas. It is my own personal monument to the integrity of the word on the page: palpable vicarious experience free from consumerist coercion.

What Were They Thinking?

As long as artists have drawn, painted, and sculpted the human figure, they have sought models to pose for them. In the art history to which we have been taught to pay attention, most of the artists are men, most of their models women. Some women have derived a modest fame posing for famous artists; they've entered our consciousness as muses. This was true of Camille Claudel, who was Auguste Rodin's favorite model; Berthe Morisot, who posed for Édouard Manet; and Dora Maar, who sat for many of Pablo Picasso's canvases. Often the artist/model relationship was complicated or exploitative, as with Paul Gauguin's Polynesian women.

Claudel was an artist in her own right and a very talented one. During her lifetime, though, she was only really known as the subject of her lover's work. Georgia O'Keeffe and Frida Kahlo were also extraordinary artists. First known as muses to the photographer Alfred Stieglitz and muralist Diego Rivera, respectively, in time their art became as revered as that of their husbands if not more so. It's no coincidence that O'Keeffe and Kahlo lived in the twentieth century, when women artists were beginning to be noticed. When women were beginning to be noticed. And I don't want to leave this as a passive statement. They still had to be twice as talented and work twice as hard to gain that modicum of attention that would eventually lead to recognition.

What were they thinking, these models sitting in long silence while men traced their images on canvas or in stone? Were the silences broken by conversations beyond "Turn just a bit more to the right" or "Keep your lips parted, please" or possibly even "Do you need a break?" Were any of them imagining their own hand on brush or chisel, their own choice of color and form? Or were most thinking of hearth and children, what to make for their family's next meal, how good it would be to put their clothes back on?

In my early twenties, I earned a bit of extra money modeling for art classes at the University of New Mexico. One of these was Herb Goldman's sculpture studio. Another was a course taught by visiting professor Elaine de Kooning, the friend and mentor I later followed to New York. Elaine could tell that I longed to hold that piece of charcoal or paintbrush myself, try my own hand at reproduction instead of modeling, be subject rather than object. After the first session, she tore off a length of brown paper from a large roll and told me to have a go. A quarter century later, during my immigration trial in El Paso, Texas, the government attorney accused me of "modeling nude for art classes in the 1950s." The implication: I was a whore. I never became a visual artist, but that moment in which Elaine urged me to try my hand at it was an important waystation on my journey toward independent agency.

Artists, mostly men but increasingly also women, produce iconic images or prototypes of those figures we've come to identify with a particular time or culture. A millennium and a half before our era, Nefertiti was the Great Royal Wife of the Egyptian Pharaoh Akhenaten. Because it was discovered in his workshop, her painted bust is said to have been crafted by the artist Thutmose in 1345 BCE. As a child, I often heard Nefertiti described as the most beautiful woman in the world and, indeed, her classic likeness became my reference for female looks. Thutmose is not a name most people would know today, but Nefertiti's is known throughout the world.

The multifaceted Italian artist Leonardo da Vinci painted the *Mona Lisa* in 1503. It is the most famous female likeness in Western art, considered a pivotal work of the Italian Renaissance. Lisa del Giocondo is believed to have been the model. We know that da Vinci was gay, so the model/artist relationship was probably safely professional. The *Mona Lisa* is perhaps the most visited, most written-about, most sung-about, and most parodied work of art that has ever been exhibited in a museum. The model's countenance is quiet, her mouth projecting an ever-so-faint smile. While Nefertiti's beauty is proud, commanding, I have always found it hard to understand Lisa del Giocondo's attraction.

Sometime around 1665, the Dutch Golden Age painter Johannes Vermeer made a portrait of a young girl wearing a pearl earring. The likeness came to be known as *Girl with a Pearl Earring*. The model was employed as a servant in the artist's home. From the moment he took her as his model, she probably fulfilled that need rather than cooking and cleaning. She may also have been Vermeer's lover. Centuries later, their alliance would inspire a novel and then a film. We can be sure that neither occurred to the young unnamed subject; motion pictures weren't even dreamed of in her time. As she posed for the master, she may have been telling herself that these sessions were infinitely easier than housework. Or maybe not. Maybe, like all young women at the beck and call of older men, she worried about his possible next move.

Shortly before his death, the Spanish painter Diego Velázquez produced his famous *Infanta Margarita Teresa in a Blue Dress* in 1659. The young girl is decked out in a lavish outfit that looks like it weighs twice what she does. This painting is typical of those commissioned by members of the European courts: the model's character or personality sometimes managing to breathe through such trappings of royalty. I imagine that little Margarita Teresa endured her sittings patiently. She was, after all, groomed for such demands.

A century and a half later, Francisco Goya made two paintings of the same woman in identical pose, one nude, the other clothed. They are known as *La maja desnuda* and *La maja vestida*. At the time, painting nude women in Spain was frowned upon, and Goya was brought before the Inquisitional Court for questioning. We don't have a record of the proceedings so don't know what transpired, but the twin images have been revered ever since. The word *maja* means a woman of the lower class. It is believed that the model for both paintings, which now hang side by side at the Museo Nacional del Prado in Madrid, was Pepita Tudó, Goya's lover. What was she thinking as she lay on that couch? In each of the canvases, there is a flicker of difference in her expression; she seems slightly more at ease in the naked version.

There are artists who deform or fragment their models' images. Such was the case with many of Spanish artist Pablo Picasso's women. His famous *Three Figures*, painted in 1921, depicts three women. They are sturdy and heavyset. Two are standing while one is seated. They are all rather passive in demeanor. One can imagine them there for no other purpose than the artist's use. Throughout his long career, Picasso used many models, men as well as women, distorting them to his will. In his cubist period he chopped his models into angles and planes. This rendered them unrecognizable but for years was the embodiment of modern art.

The Colombian painter Fernando Botero Angulo is another who distorts his models. He is known as a figurative artist, but all the people he paints are almost grotesquely fat, their enormous bodies balanced on tiny feet. Botero paints men as well as women in this way, but his depictions of women clash more obviously with the ideal of female beauty. His style is known as Boterism. His enlarged body parts represent political criticism, sometimes humor. Asked why he developed this particular style, he said: "You adopt a position intuitively; only later do you attempt to rationalize or even justify it."

Botero isn't the first artist whose work exaggerates or distorts the human form. The Greek painter, sculptor, and architect of the Spanish Renaissance Doménikos Theotokópoulos, better known as El Greco, elongated his painted figures. So did early twentieth-century Swiss sculptor Alberto Giacometti. Irish artist Francis Bacon stretched and compressed his models into his unique vision. U.S. American Grant Wood claimed instant fame with his painting *American Gothic*, which shows a farmhouse in his native Iowa with a long narrow window. Standing before that window is a a man and a woman, of whose elongated faces the artist said: "I imagined American Gothic people with their faces stretched out long to go with this American Gothic house." Wood's models were his sister and his dentist, whom he portrayed as a farmer and his daughter, dressing them as if they were "tintypes from my old family album." The mark of an artist has often been to project the human figure not as we see it but as his or her passion wants to tell the story.

Great portraiture has been done by photographers as well as painters. Dorothea Lange's "Migrant Mother," made in 1936 when the U.S. American photographer was documenting the Great Depression, is one such image. We now know the subject's name: Florence Owens Thompson. In the well-known portrait she looks past the camera's lens, embodying the essence of her poverty and despair. The two children nestled beside her are turned completely away. We do not even see their faces.

Many male artists painted their mothers. James McNeill Whistler did so in 1871. He called the portrait *Arrangement in Grey and Black No. 1*, but it is known today as Whistler's Mother. The twentieth-century Dutch painter Willem de Kooning painted his mother over and over again; she is believed to have been the woman he was thinking of when he made his series of women in the mid-1950s. While the figures are abstracted beyond any easy recognition of the female form, one can nevertheless find the voracious gaping mouth and fierce demeanor he so feared in his childhood. Willem's wife, my friend Elaine de Kooning, was also known for her portraits. She painted dozens of men and women, famous and friends, young and old. Each is a masterpiece. I am fortunate that she did seven small black-and-white painted sketches of me. I can't remember what I was thinking as I sat for those pictures. We were probably gossiping about the art world as we tended to do.

When I arrived in New York City in the late summer of 1958, I got a job posing for an artist named Leon Golub. He wanted me nude but always painted me in an imagined ballerina tutu. Golub was polite and kind. After each morning's two-hour session, he gave me a glass of freshly squeezed orange juice and sent me on my way with five dollars. I no longer remember what went through my mind during those sittings.

What Were They Thinking?

What were they thinking, these muses of famous artists, as they were being drawn, painted, or sculpted? What was I thinking in the stillness of those hours in which I posed for art classes in New Mexico and New York? In most cases I cannot remember. All I know is that, in some deep recess of my being, I longed to be the artist, not the subject.

In time, I made the transition.

Silliness Gene

As I write, my wife and I have been with one another thirty-four years. We've been living together since 1986 but were only able to legalize our union in 2013 when marriage equality became the law. We couldn't have imagined that the civil ceremony would move us as much as it did. One detail we remember with delight was standing in line to get our license at Brooklyn's City Hall. A couple of very large African American women were cutting it up in the line ahead of us. They and their contingent of friends were having a grand old time. One wore a baseball cap studded with outrageous buttons. Their joy, their silliness, were contagious. It seemed to combine the expression of a love that until recently had been outlawed with a healthy dose of being able to create a party from any situation.

Barbara and I have worked hard at a relationship we both feel immensely fortunate to have found, and there are many aspects of it that make it solid. Commitment. Trust. Transparency. The artist's eye and love of one another's work. Mutual support. Generosity of spirit. Dependability. Agreement on life's major issues. And a general easiness in the comings and goings of daily life. But if you asked us to name a particularly important aspect of our relationship, I suspect we'd both say silliness.

Silliness is difficult to define, hard to put into words. You have it or you don't. If you have it, you don't need it explained. And if you don't have it, no attempt at explanation seems to work. It's not about trivialization or clownishness. Playfulness is definitely involved. Silliness often includes a banter only the two of us find funny. Sometimes it causes us to shake with laughter, descend into paroxysms of delight, tears spilling from our eyes. It's at once unexpected and necessary. And extremely intimate. It is a behavior that draws us close, alleviates pain, and occasionally makes use of a dark humor we can only indulge with one another because anyone else might interpret it as sexist, racist, xenophobic, or incurring some other stance we vehemently reject. We can make that sort of joke with each other because we know we are not stepping into those cesspools but rather mocking those who do. Perhaps we are exorcising a biased upbringing by meeting it right where it lives and laughing in its bully face.

As we age, our hearing suffers. This can be annoying but also provides material for raucous exchanges. Our misheard comments easily contribute to bouts of silliness. One of us exclaiming, "Oh my god, I thought you said *seventy dildos walking*," or the other hearing "Play with yourself" when the suggestion was "Take care of your health," are miscommunications guaranteed to crack us both up. Other age-related missteps almost always conjure a silliness response rather than exasperation or grumpiness. It's about repurposing disability as playfulness.

We wonder if we were born with a silliness gene, or if our vastly different social conditioning—Barbara had to overcome a working-class conservative and religiously fundamentalist background; I an upper middle-class liberal one—has nevertheless joined us at the hip.

When we met, most of our friends were surprised by the immediacy of our mutual attraction. Desire unleashed itself in torrents. Over the years, we've settled into quieter rhythms, but the intensity remains. When one of us has been away for a while, the other invariably suffers from a lack of silliness. When we're back together and the silliness returns, we both experience immense relief. Just as easily, when one of us falls ill, silliness may become the victim of pain, low energy, or exhaustion. We miss it then.

We enjoy friends who are silly, even about momentous things, although we have many treasured friends who lack the gene. But those who take themselves or a situation too seriously tend to annoy or bore us. This is true even when we're talking about inhumane political policies, war, disrespect for women and minorities, criminal immigration practices, bullying, and other brutalities. It's not that we don't feel the seriousness of the situation. We do, and deeply. But if we can't change it, we might as well laugh about it. Dark humor is a release. Why? I can't really say.

I wish I could give an example, one that would make clear what silliness is and how it functions. How we use but don't abuse it, the invisible line we won't cross. There is a sort of sophistication involved. It's hard, because the example itself might reduce or invalidate the concept. When you try to share a private joke, you'll find yourself spending twice the time trying to explain why it was funny. And still, no one is laughing.

Maybe I should talk about cultures where I've noticed that silliness seems to be part of the fabric of everyday life. One of these, perhaps astonishingly, is Vietnam. In the fall of 1974, six months before the end of the U.S. American war in that country, I was invited by the North Vietnamese

Women's Union to travel the length of the northern half. Vietnam was divided then, and the north was firmly in Communist hands.

I was taken by jeep from Hanoi all the way down to the 17th Parallel and into the liberated zone of Quảng Tri, stopping along the way to speak with women who commanded anti-aircraft artillery, those who'd spent years in the underground tunnels, and young women whose husbands and brothers were on the front lines. My goal was to write a book about Vietnamese women in struggle. I was given a guide and a translator.

Often, I listened to my hosts talking among themselves. They laughed more than I expected. Could they be telling jokes in the midst of this tragic war? When I asked, they translated, trying hard to explain what had been so funny. One joke involved bombs "descending like turds." They looked at me, perhaps expecting me to join in their laughter. I must have looked nonplussed. Only years later did I understand that these Vietnamese comrades were using dark humor and silliness to defuse the daily tension in which they lived.

When Barbara, who taught middle school for twenty years, would tell me about a joke one of her Navajo students had pulled, I identified the silliness component in his humor. Maybe silliness is a way some groups who live with constant hardship deal with that pain. I understand its utility now.

It is said that desperate times call for desperate measures.

Silliness may be to despair what social struggle is to the frustration of witnessing the destruction of our good earth and the devastation of its peoples. We haven't yet been able to reverse the trend, so we hope silliness will take up the slack.

What Would They Say?

A WORLDWIDE PANDEMIC MADE ME THINK of those family members and friends I have loved who are no longer here. Perhaps because I expected the virus would take many. If, as predicted, the death toll reached into the millions, some would likely be people close to me. I might even be one of them. I am thinking today of some friends who have been spared this crisis, with all its anguish, fear, and uncertainty. I hear their voices now and imagine what each might have said.

My father would have been obstinately optimistic. It was always his way. Perhaps because he truly believed things would work out; perhaps because he felt his role was to convince others of that. Mother would have worried about every aspect of the situation, sharing every bit of advice to which she was privy, possibly disappearing into total isolation. They both lived through the Spanish flu of 1918, but Dad was twelve and Mother eight, so they were probably too young to have experienced the collective anxiety, although even as children they must have sensed something dire was happening. My sister Ann died several years ago. Often anxious, she might have suffered this crisis more than most. I am glad none of them is here to confront the current terror.

I am certain Meridel LeSueur would have reminded us that this is not the first crisis of this magnitude we have survived, nor will it be the last. Meridel, I hear you again speaking of history's pendulum, telling us how it swings inevitably from horror to reconciliation and back. Poet of the prairie and socialist ideals, you possessed a long-range understanding of life and struggle. You would have taken lessons from this dangerous situation and kept us focused on justice. You would have gone along with social distancing, but you surely would have prioritized social solidarity. I miss your calm, your wise eyes and experienced voice.

Maidu poet Janice Gould, gone from us in 2019, would also have had something meaningful to say about our current dilemma. But while Meridel would have spoken in rousing tones, you, Janice, would have given us a more intimate message—just as memorable but touching upon the ideas and feelings we unearth through observation and quiet contemplation. I'm sure you would have linked traditional tribal wisdom with what life taught you as a mixed-blood lesbian poet, daughter of a Native woman and trans father who became Barbara late in life. Janice, I wish I could read one last poem of yours, linking your own history with what we are juggling today and inspiring us to keep a place for hope.

Laurette Séjourné, you left so many years ago that I wonder if I can still speak to you now. How long does memory persist after death? How long may we continue to converse? Our connection seems too powerful for it to simply disappear. You taught me so much when we were close, during those rich and turbulent Mexican years and later when you visited me in Cuba. And you offered those lessons in a way I can't forget, declaring your ideas resolutely, as if they were scientific truths, then waiting for my hesitant response before assessing which parts of the whole you would have to repeat or clarify so I might understand. Yet always with love, always with love.

Mark Behr, thinking of you I relive my initial refusal to meet you, then how I relented and came to love you beyond measure; your very life personified the human capacity for absolution. My brother of unrelenting brilliance, I have no doubt that you would have had plenty to say right now. And none of it would have been what one expects to emerge in the midst of a crisis such as this. You somehow made everything new. We would have laughed and cried together. You would have made surprising connections, and every one of them would have put me in touch with some aspect of life or myself that blooms the moment your voice articulates it. Dear Mark, how I miss you now and always!

Elaine de Kooning, you would have smiled as you embraced family and friends. You would have smiled a lot, even finding unexpected reasons to laugh out loud. You would have made outrageous jokes, then stopped for a moment to make sure we knew you understood the serious underbelly of this situation, while acting to help everyone with whom you came in contact. And you would have come in contact with all sorts: friends and acquaintances, street people and buyers of art. Social distancing just wasn't in your nature. Your exuberance would have been more contagious than any virus. Had you not left us more than thirty years ago, you might have been one of those felled by this plague; you were, after all, a heavy smoker, and your lungs may well have proven vulnerable. As it turned out, you were spared this moment of dread.

And Michael Ratner. Oh Michael, how we could use your brilliance and commitment now! That might be what first comes to mind when I think about your life: how an incisive legal mind and committed activist came together in the same man. I can still feel that small parenthesis of peace in the midst of war as we floated lazily on the Great Lake of Nicaragua, 1983: two friends in a rowboat cutting a swatch of time from disaster. And a couple of years later, when I realized the government would initiate deportation proceedings against me, how my first call was to you. Your immediate assurance that you would take my case planted a seed of hope unbroken until we won. Your work must have been as pivotal for everyone you defended. Your unique and comforting spirit accompanies me today.

Eleni Bastea, you were far away when you died, in a place where you could receive the treatments you needed and also fulfill a fellowship that gave you joy. I'm so glad you had the chance to have that fellowship as long as you did. You who gave so much thought to place and dislocation would surely have had something to say about the virus's disorienting nature. Oh yes. You missed it by mere weeks, but the last text you wrote and shared with me spoke eloquently of memory and place. Painfully thin and dying, you gave to the very end. I am glad you didn't have to fear this new menace along with the struggle you were already waging with such courage.

Dear Rini Price, also recently departed, you would have looked sideways then back again, assumed the pensive expression you so often had, then set about to make the perfect pencil drawing. I can see you now: your gaze beyond our line of sight, your hand and drawing implement seemingly effortless as they moved across the paper. Yours was a wry commentary on the human condition. "The Species," you called us, and we knew exactly what you meant. Even in the fog that enveloped your final months, you would have found a way to communicate a bit of that creative wisdom that characterized who you were. I only hope we would have been able to listen.

I imagine a chorus of voices, too many to recreate here.

But I hear you all, repurposing the gifts you offered in life.

//
Starfish on the Beach: A Fable for 2020[1]

I THINK OF A STORY Barbara used to tell, about a man standing on a beach scattered with hundreds of starfish. He picked them up, one by one, and threw each back into the sea. Another man walking by—such stories always seem to feature men—stopped, watched for a while, then said: "You'll never be able to throw them all back. Do you think what you're doing really matters?" The first man picked up another starfish, tossed it into the waves, and answered: "Mattered to that one."

I'm thinking of this story now in the context of COVID-19, the plague that is sickening and killing people around the world. I've heard it suggested, both by those who believe in science and by Christian fundamentalists, that this is

---

1. First published in *Starfish on a Beach: The Pandemic Poems*, Wings Press, 2020. Also published in *Estrellas de mar sobre una playa: los poemas de la pandemia / Starfish on a Beach: The Pandemic Poems*, co-edition Editorial Abisinia and Escarabajo Editorial, 2020.

a culling. The Earth is cleansing itself of overpopulation, ridding itself of surplus humans, as it were. The Christian fundamentalists would substitute the word *God* for the word *Earth*.

Which leads to my next thought. Even if we can't save everyone who gets sick, we must do our best to protect as many as possible. It may not matter to everyone, but it will surely matter to those who survive.

On the Gender Spectrum

TO BEGIN, LET ME SAY that I know I will be entering risky territory here. I am not a transgender person but a white, middle-class lesbian. I was not born into the wrong body and do not presume to speak for people who are. I cede the final word on the subject to those who have made the difficult journey to their true gender or feel the need to do so. But, just as I know a diverse range of such people—those who have transitioned as completely as possible, those who have chosen not to take hormones or undergo surgeries, those who assume an androgynous identity, and those for whom cross-dressing is an acceptable compromise—I believe all of us who think about this complex issue have a right to utter an opinion. Those who are not poor write about poverty, after all. Those born in this country express our views on immigration, often with interesting things to say. Everyone needs thoughtful allies. At the very least, may this text open a conversation. In all humility, I confess that my opinions include many more questions than answers.

Women born in a male body long to present as who they really are. Men who are born in a female body long for the same. I honor that. A biological male who knows she is a woman becomes one physically through hormonal treatments and finally surgery. Presenting as female now, she may bloom in the woman's body she presumed would be heterosexual, or perhaps realize she is a lesbian; sometimes there are further surprises. Someone born in a woman's body has always known he is a man. Through hormone treatments and surgeries, he makes the transition. In whatever direction, such change requires psychological work as well; the adjustment is dramatic. Many of these transitions work, while some end up not satisfying the person searching for mind/body consonance. I honor them all, feel joy for those who find comfort in their decision to inhabit a body that finally fits, and am deeply sad for those who don't.

We may ask the question: is gender biological or psychological or both? If we recognize the mind/body connection, we are likely to say both. But how much one and how much the other? And how might cultural mores and social rejection or acceptance alter the equation?

In recent years the term *non-binary* has come into frequent use. Those who claim the identification refuse to be categorized as male or female, for generations the only two gender possibilities permissible in our culture. Over my lifetime and at least in some places, *lesbian*, *homosexual*, *bisexual*, *queer*, *transgender*, and *intersex* have been added to the list. In the more enlightened cultures, these eight identities are now recognized as legitimate. Within certain indigenous communities, there has always been a place for those of indeterminate or dual gender expression; they have been called *two-spirit people*. This amplification of the recognition of gender difference is welcome, but I believe that all these categories fall woefully short of all the gender identities that do in fact exist. *Non-binary* barely scratches the surface of who we are. I believe there are as many different gender identities as there are human beings.

And why limit this observation to humans? Throughout the animal world, we observe an extraordinarily broad range of sexual identities and practices: same sex, so-called opposite sex, animals who possess both male and female genitalia and assume each identity as needed at different times in their lives, and asexual animals who nevertheless reproduce via other means.

A sidebar to this discussion is the spurious way in which right-wing interests have used difference to spark the culture wars that help move the political needle their way. Stigmatizing certain people as "other" has always been the practice of authoritarian regimes and a good way to encourage and take advantage of the racist, homophobic, and xenophobic attitudes long festering in our society. Throughout our history, we can see how this attitude has claimed victims, from Native Americans, African Americans, Hispanics, Middle Easterners, and those of Asian descent to the sexually or gender-different, immigrants, teenage mothers, and those who have lost home or welfare. During the Second World War, Japanese and German Americans were ostracized and, in the case of the former, confined to prison camps. After September 11, 2001, Arabs and anyone who looked Arabic bore the brunt of our nation's fear and rage. Right now, immigrants and transgender people are among the primary targets of officialdom's disdain.

For transgender women and men, the public restroom scandal of a few years back was but one example of such disdain.[1] Causing people to feel less than and taunting them

---

1. In 2016, the U.S. Department of Justice and U.S. Department of Education, under President Barack Obama, issued "guidance" to state and private educational institutions declaring that these institutions had

under the aegis of some fabricated moral code have resulted in untold misery and no few deaths. Since 2015, the Human Rights Campaign has tracked ever-increasing violence against transgender people. So far, the year 2020 has seen more than two dozen such hate crimes resulting in death in the U.S. alone, the majority of them Black transgender women. These fatalities do not include those by suicide or from being denied employment, being forced into sex work, or the inability to access appropriate healthcare. These crimes alone should make us acknowledge the terrible prejudice that exists against transgender people.

And the negative targeting of transgender people in particular has been practiced not only by the right. Our own communities have too often been guilty of such behavior. I am thinking, among other shameful moments, of the Michigan Womyn's Music Festival some years back, when transgender women were not considered worthy of admittance. They weren't deemed "real" women.[2] In the same period, transgender men were frequently accused of transitioning in order to benefit from male privilege

---

to allow transgender students to use toilets according to their gender identity. But struggles around who would be allowed to use which public restroom continue today, especially in the southern United States.

2. The Michigan Womyn's Music Festival was a feminist women's event held annually from 1976 to 2015 on privately owned land in Oceana County, Michigan. The event was built, staffed, run, and attended exclusively by women with girls, boys, and toddlers permitted. In 2014, the festival announced a policy of admitting only "womyn-born women," thereby excluding transgender women. This led Equality Michigan to boycott the festival and drew criticism from the Human Rights Campaign, GLAAD, the National Center for Lesbian Rights, and the National LGBTQ Task Force. The following year was the last for the event.

rather than because they had been born in the wrong body. Judgment from the outside is risky and inevitably suspect.

As I say, I honor the choices people make for their lives, the identities they assume, and the tremendous courage it takes—especially in a society as religiously dominated as ours—to deliberately embark upon a journey to change one's biological birth identity. Such decisions are not taken lightly; they involve risk and pain. To live in contradiction with one's physical body must be like living out of balance every day of one's life, but remedying that situation is complex and difficult. I believe the counseling, hormone treatments, electrolysis, and surgical interventions necessary to effect the needed change should be honored, aided, and free and universally available, as I believe all healthcare should be.

At the same time, I feel the need to say that the personal misery, the horror of finding oneself in the wrong physical body, the danger to one's health of hormone treatments and corrective surgeries: none of these might be necessary if society allowed each person to be who he, she, or they are. Clearly, some would still feel the need to transition physically, and that should be their prerogative. But if we understood that in truth we are all non-binary, and that the labels thrust upon us have not worked for our benefit but have steered us to comply with stereotypes pushed by most major religions and that make obscene amounts of money for the fashion and cosmetic industries, plastic surgery practitioners, beauty contests, and charm schools, some of us might be spared the risks.

In other words, what if the need for gender reassignment is largely a product of our culture's failure to recognize individuality rather than force it into narrow molds? Society itself should change; this shouldn't be the responsibility of individuals who do not fit a prescribed gender presentation.

Time can redress the agony, albeit much too slowly. We know of historical figures who have lived a different gender presentation because they felt they were born into the wrong body, or loved someone of their own gender, in order to fight in a war or take up a profession. Sometimes the disguise was revealed only at the person's death, surprising even their intimates. We remember a female pope, said to be the reason why all subsequent popes are forced to submit to an examination to make sure they possess male genitalia.[3] And the story of Virginia Woolf's Orlando is a metaphor for difference down through the centuries.[4]

What today is punishable by death in some societies is gradually finding acceptance in others. One hundred years from now, if humanity survives, we may be able to accept difference along the complex spectrum of gender. After all, it is tragic when the solution to society's prejudices is considered the responsibility only of vulnerable individuals.

I speak my thoughts mindful that I may be attacked by those who live a reality I cannot know. And I take comfort in Galileo, who understood that to speak against the dogma of the Church—the maximum authority in his time—was to risk condemnation or worse. But Galileo did speak,

---

3. Pope Joan (Ioannes Anglicus; 855–857) was, according to legend, a woman who reigned as pope for a few years during the Middle Ages. She is said to have taken the name John VIII. Her story first appeared in chronicles in the thirteenth century and subsequently spread throughout Europe. It was widely believed for centuries, but most modern scholars regard it as fictional. Nevertheless, it has been used to strengthen the belief among the Catholic hierarchy that only men may lead the Church.

4. Virginia Woolf's novel *Orlando* was based on the author's love affair with Vita Sackville-West. Its protagonist reappears throughout time, always with an identity that challenges gender stereotypes. The novel has also been made into a motion picture.

and today his discoveries are lauded and accepted as good science. He also knew when to remain silent, conscious that doing so would give him the freedom to continue his work. I have yet to learn to cultivate such silence.

Art and Technology through Time and Space

A COUPLE OF EXPERIENCES CAME TOGETHER at the end of 2020 that had me pondering writing and communication—globally, back through history, and cross-culturally—as well as other artistic genres, as they are impacted by technology. My son Gregory and two other professors at the University of the Republic in Uruguay (UDELAR) offered a class in fall 2020 on art and technology. Attendees were equally divided between artists and engineers. My grandson, Martín, an engineer like his father, was one of these. I was able to virtually sit in on a session that focused on art and technology in communication, at which Gregory gave an introduction to the topic and Martín and another student made a presentation. Around the same time, my wife Barbara and I happened to watch two episodes of *Nova* devoted to the history of writing. They are called "A to Z: The First Alphabet" and "A to Z: How Writing Changed the World." I want to begin these notes by acknowledging the contributions made by Gregory and Martín Randall and Barbara Byers. I am, of course, solely responsible for where my intuition takes me.

The fortuitous intersection of these *Nova* episodes and Gregory's class has me thinking about writing and other artistic genres as communication, and how communication itself changes over time. How advances in technology have facilitated and shaped these changes, and how artistic vision overlaps and informs them. These considerations also have me pondering the many issues that emanate from this history, such as how writing developed in different cultures and at different times; how medieval copyists and later mechanical methods of reproduction affected access to information, creating literate and illiterate classes of people; the relationship between communication and art as exemplified in everything from the ancient cave paintings uncovered in various parts of southern Europe to the Maya glyphs with their sculptural definition in what are now Guatemala, Honduras, and Mexico; the Maya codices, only five of which survived the Spanish Conquest; the richly illuminated manuscripts of the Middle Ages; mural movements in different countries and different times; industrial design; the thousands of typefaces created and used today; and how political conflicts have produced both propaganda and all-but-unbreakable codes, just to name a few. From early in our history and so-called "pre-history,"[1] there have been classes of people who had greater or lesser access to knowledge. Technology—from the ability to make fire to the development of weaving, ceramics, metals, and navigational and communication systems, among others—

---

1. I reject the idea that history began with the invention of writing. I prefer the notion that human life on earth has traveled one continuous history punctuated by events that sent it in different directions and enabled it to make great social and cultural leaps.

has consistently brought more people into the illustrated realm.

I have long been struck by how writing developed simultaneously and often along similar lines in areas of the world distant from one another and without any conceivable contact between them.[2] In some places it took the form of cuneiform writing or hieroglyphics (symbols combining logographic, syllabic, and alphabetic elements). In other places what we now call letters represented sounds. Because human development has followed the same trajectory almost everywhere, or for some other reason we have not yet been able to decipher, similar solutions were often applied to similar problems.

For example, the rebus feature was common to both Chinese and Egyptian, languages that apparently have a marked correspondence even now. The rebus is a symbol, often preceding a letter or pictogram, that indicates what area of life it describes. A pictogram that may be read as both sadness and a tree may be understood to refer to a tree when it is preceded by a mark common to forests. This sort of clue can also be found in the Maya glyphs. Another commonality is the way numbers have influenced language

---

2. Leroi Gourhan (1911-1986), a French archaeologist, paleontologist, and anthropologist, wrote brilliantly about the relationship between the technical (which he described as universal tendency) and the ethnic (as specific, differentiated concretization). He paid a good deal of attention to how diverse cultures in different parts of the world arrived at similar discoveries and inventions when there could not have been any contact between them. Crucial to his understanding of human evolution is the notion that the transition to bipedality freed the hands for grasping and the face for gesturing and speaking such that the development of the cortex, technology, and language all follow from the adoption of an upright stance. He posited a third kind of memory (in addition to the genetic memory contained in DNA and the individual memory of the nervous system) and thus a new form of anticipation or programming.

development. Number sequences can be found in ancient writing systems, but the most obvious relationship today is the digital use of the binary system of zero and one.

If we think of communication not only in its written form but in its spoken, visual, and gestural ones, we come to issues such as the importance of orality and body language in preserving cultures from one generation to the next; the great variety of pedagogies that have been developed in teaching at all levels; painting; sculpture; photography; political oratory; religious sermons; myths; allegories; advertising; diaries and recipe books (where much women's writing was found hiding before our work was deemed acceptable for wider publication); poetry; genres involving humor such as comics, cartoons, and jokes; song; drama and opera across cultures and throughout history; the telling of bedtime stories and other oral practices that inform the nature of parenting; and even such uniquely rich variations as the many sign languages used by the Deaf and hearing impaired in which three-dimensional expression necessarily substitutes for the voice. Or braille, where touching an arrangement of raised dots allows communication. The artform of mime also comes to mind.

Science fiction and other artistic genres reveal each generation's imagination of what the future may be like, and it is interesting to see how a state of being that was futuristic for our grandparents may look like everyday life to us. Think of Leonardo da Vinci's notebooks, in which we find drawings of diving suits, machine guns, elevators, airplanes, and other inventions that came into being centuries after the artist's death. Fast-forward from da Vinci, we have George Orwell, Marge Piercy, and Margaret Atwood, all of whom wrote frighteningly prophetic books projecting situations that have become all too real today. The intersection between art and technology isn't linear but moves backward and forward in time.

Through the long span of human experience, grandmothers and grandfathers have instructed mothers and fathers, who have in turn instructed their children, on how to be human via verbal directives and setting non-verbal but nonetheless powerful examples. *Human* has often meant *moral*, with a nod to the ethics of a particular time and place. In a deeper sense, *human* means just that: a person who is a responsible agent in relationship with other persons, with the sensibility and ability to experience emotions and make choices that characterize the human as different from other animals.

Visual art, too, is a form of language. I think of the cave paintings, the religious art of the Middle Ages (how stained-glass windows and statuary in European churches functioned like picture books telling the stories of the Bible to those who frequented them), the great mosaic and mural traditions, and all the breakthrough art movements such as the Renaissance, mannerism, baroque, rococo, neoclassicism, romanticism, cubism, impressionism, surrealism, Dadaism, abstract expressionism, minimalism, and pop art, among others. Each reflects the sociopolitical characteristics of a place and time and the artist's response to that moment. We can say the same of music, theater, dance, and all the other arts.

Spoken languages are unique in that they run the risk of extinction when the groups that speak them become too small to ensure their survival. When the last speaker is gone, the language cannot be revived. Right now, a third of the world's languages have fewer than one thousand speakers left. Of the world's seven thousand recognized languages, one dies out every two weeks. By the end of the next century, fifty to ninety percent of them are predicted to disappear. My friend Bob Holman, the poet and cultural organizer, spent years tracking down at-risk languages in Wales and Australia, recording elders who were still alive and could speak the language or dialect in question.[3] Many specialists today are dedicated to saving endangered languages.

In all societies, we must ask ourselves: who communicates? Who is permitted to communicate? If the only voices we hear are those of the conquerors and owners, our knowledge of the world is skewed. In recent times, we have begun to be able to hear the voices of women, minorities, lesbians, gay men, transgender people, immigrants, those with mental or physical disabilities, the very young, and the very old. This has expanded our ability to know the world as it is, but some groups are inevitably relegated or ignored. There are always new groups from which we need to hear. Additionally, making space for these voices often follows a trend or fad; publishing them may be an effort to capitalize economically on a momentary fascination. The U.S. academic literary canon, for example, is still overwhelmingly male, white, and upper class; the canon in no way mirrors the full range of all those who have written brilliantly in the past or are doing so today. Separate courses may feature women, Native American, Black, Hispanic, and LGBTQ writers, but these are unlikely to be included as basic texts or gain their place in the canon.

Throughout history, some repressed groups developed specialized languages that allowed them to maneuver in dangerous territory because of gender or other inequalities. One of these languages was Nüshu, based on the standard Chinese script, Hanzi, but with far fewer syllables and

---

3. *Language Matters*, the film conceived of and co-produced by Bob Holman, premiered at the National Museum of the American Indian on January 21, 2015, and aired on PBS that same month. It was filmed around the world, including on a remote island off the coast of Australia where four hundred Aboriginal people speak ten different at-risk languages, in Wales where once-endangered Welsh is now making a comeback, and in Hawaii where Hawaiians are fighting to save their native tongue.

spoken exclusively by women in Jiangyong County in Hunan province in the south of China. Nüshu is believed to have been developed as early at the thirteenth and fourteenth centuries, reaching its peak expression around the middle of the seventeenth. Some years back, I read about the last woman alive who was able to communicate in Nüshu. Scholars were rushing to record what they could of what she remembered.

In the United States, many Native tribes have rich linguistic histories that were largely ignored by outsiders. Governmental edict even forbade speaking them to greet or pray as the U.S. took tribal lands, disrespected cultures and in some cases all but obliterated them, and demanded only English at reservation schools. Hidden traditions or syncretism replaced the fullness of native traditions. Condescension passed itself off as aid, denying whole nations their cultural rights. Similar histories exist in Canada and Australia. Today, many tribes are preserving their languages by teaching them at their own schools and by publishing literature in their native tongues. The latter is often produced in the original with facing-page translations. For all languages, expert translation is an important area of cultural communication. Despite its unfortunate relegation within the literary world, it is an artform in and of itself.

African Americans have something called Black English, sometimes referred to as Ebonics. This is a communicative form that draws upon the language of the rural South, with its infusion of African words brought over with the slave trade and embellished with the street language of the African American working class. It first came to my attention when I taught at Trinity College in the 1980s and '90s. Several of my students asked if they could write their term papers in Black English. I said yes, then struggled to be able to read and comment on them. Once I gained a modest comprehension, I was able to appreciate the dialect's richness of expression.

The vast number of immigrants to the United States from Spanish-speaking countries often develop a sort of "Spanglish," combining words and expressions in the particular way the language from their countries of origin mix with the new language they are absorbing here. This can be heard in poetry as well as in everyday speech. In fact, every language spoken by a large enough group of immigrants enriches the language of the host country. I remain convinced that officially sanctioned English or any other language, that which is approved by a country's Academy of the Language for example, is limiting rather than creative. New words and expressions enter every language constantly.

Colonialists tried, and for generations succeeded, in killing a profusion of indigenous languages. They repeatedly used religion as a cover for such practice. Alternately, they may claim to be preserving the native tongue even as colonialism subverts its culture. The Summer Institute of Linguistics, based in Norman, Oklahoma, has for years sent specialists throughout the world to translate the New Testament and use it to proselytize and convert. Disturbingly, many of its translators are so competent they have been hired onto secular projects and have managed to inject them with their Christian worldview. Increasingly, native speakers are challenging this practice.

I remember with shame that, in the 1960s, when Mexican poet Sergio Mondragón and I edited *El Corno Emplumado / The Plumed Horn*, a bilingual literary journal out of Mexico City, we published several indigenous writers simply as "primitive poets" without even distinguishing them by name or tribe. Today we are witnessing a corrective to this kind of diminution. More and more indigenous literature is being published, though not nearly enough attention is given it.

Joy Harjo, an enrolled member of the Mvskoke tribe and currently U.S. poet laureate for a third term, recently edited *When the Light of the World Was Subdued, Our Songs Came Through* (Norton, 2020), an anthology of 160 native poets representing many nations through several generations. It is an extraordinary collection, but it is perhaps telling that it was only published once we had an indigenous poet laureate.

Mexico's National Autonomous University (UNAM) holds a fascinating poetry event every two years or so. It is called Lenguas de America (American Languages). Twelve poets are invited to read their work: one each from the European languages of the continent—Spanish, French, English, and Portuguese—and eight others representing Nahuatl, Mayan, Quechua, Aymara, Tzotzil, Guaraní, Mapuche, Seri, or any of the hundreds of other indigenous languages spoken the length and breadth of the Americas. I was invited as the poet writing in English to this revelatory event on two occasions, first in 2006 and then again in 2013. Listening to poets read their work in languages I do not understand, yet the tone and inflections of which produced a deep emotional response in me, was a very moving experience.

The story of human communication has dramatically accelerated as history has advanced. Gregory opened the class I sat in on with a brief rundown of important dates. He noted that we can trace cuneiform writing in Mesopotamia to 3400 BCE. Egyptian hieroglyphics date to around 150 years later, in 3250 BCE. The Hammurabi stone is believed to have been erected in ancient Babylonia in 1754 BCE. Incised on a diorite stele and placed in a public square, it was the first example of community communication that we know of and listed 282 laws (although only thirty or so remain visible). The Hammurabi stone was discovered for modernity in 1901 and, like so many artifacts stolen by colonialism, is on display at the Louvre in Paris.

Another key to deciphering ancient writing is the famous Rosetta Stone, also taken by colonialist plunder to the British Museum in London. The Rosetta Stone was discovered in 1799 CE by Napoleon's troops at Fort St. Julien in Egypt. It dates to 196 BCE and, because identical texts in Demotic and ancient Greek appear alongside the ancient Egyptian, has enabled scholars to read hieroglyphs. The name Rosetta now has such a deep connection to language overall that it has been given to a commercial system of language learning popular with students throughout the world.

We date Maya hieroglyphs to 300 BCE. I have stood in wonder before stone stelae covered with glyphs recording genealogies and other narratives. They seem to exude living memory, telling me that even in the presence of a language I do not know, a mysterious essence holds forth. It is as if the meaning emerges from the stone itself.

Not long after the Maya began carving their hieroglyphs, the movement of writing and communication in Europe employed copyists, artists who laboriously hand-penned onto parchment or velum (calf skin) books considered sacred by the world's main religions: Judaism, Islam, Christianity, and others. They used writing implements made from reeds and later quills extracted from birds. These books were often richly illuminated with designs that included the writing style itself. Completing a book could take a year or more. The minerals used in the colored portions of each page were imported from Asia and the Middle East; they were made from turquoise and lapis lazuli dust and the powder of other stones. Gold leaf was used lavishly.

Interestingly, this art of producing a single illuminated book on parchment followed a time when the much more plentiful and less expensive Egyptian papyrus had become increasingly unavailable after the breakup of the Roman empire. In other words, papyrus scrolls were read by great numbers of people at public libraries throughout northern Africa and Asia; think of the ancient libraries at Alexandria and Ephesus. The Roman Empire itself was known for its libraries; a mid-sized town might have twenty or thirty where people came to read literature, history, science, and other subjects. The Middle Ages brought a dramatic reduction in this accessibility. I was surprised to learn that many of the papyrus scrolls were penned by slaves, proving that many in this lowest of all classes knew how to read and write. The much more unique and elitist illuminated editions were copied by specialists from the artisan class who devoted their lives to honing complex calligraphic talents. Papyrus scrolls were the era's version of a paperback book, available for easy public consumption. A rare illuminated book might be owned by a wealthy family or kept by Church or court.

In terms of communication that traveled beyond the public square where a Socrates or some other wise man expounded orally, we can trace the ways in which messages were sent from one place to another through history and across the world. Mail was established in China as early as 900 BCE. Augustus created a state-run courier system in the first century CE. In what is now Peru, the Incas had their chaskis from the twelfth century CE. These were runners who carried messages along the Inca roads as far as 150 miles a day. By the fifteenth and sixteenth centuries, several European countries had postal services. And in 1792, the United States established the U.S. Post Office Department.

These systems enabled letters to be sent from place to place via a reliable state-run system. Here in the United States, we until quite recently considered our mail service to be absolutely trustworthy and dependable, almost sacred. Today, it shows the fissures common to so many previously trusted government departments.

The Gutenberg Bible in 1440 marked the advent of the modern printing press, eventually leading to the mass reproduction of texts. But in the eighteenth century, communication began advancing much more rapidly.

Either Samuel Morse or Alexander Popov invented the telegraph, depending on which history one chooses to believe. Both men announced their success at the end of the 1700s. Italian innovator Antonio Meucci is credited with inventing the first rudimentary telephone six decades later, in 1849. The French inventor Charles Bourseul devised a phone in 1854, but Alexander Graham Bell won the first U.S. patent for the device in 1876 and in the Western world is considered its inventor. Politics determines these "firsts," the person given credit for an invention and the date upon which it took place. I never questioned that Bell was the inventor of the telephone—I'd learned it as fact in grade school—until my children, who were educated in Cuba, were taught that it was Meucci. The widespread use of the telegraph and telephone radically changed communication.

The radio was invented in 1844 and by 1920 was in broad use throughout the developed world. I was born in 1936, and progress in mass communication speeded up even more during my lifetime. I witnessed the letterpress and linotype in action, spent hours sitting at a varitype machine or cranking the handle on a ditto and xerox. I learned several photographic print methods before graduating into the era of digital technology. In 1962, the world saw the first communication satellite. The internet as we know it came into being in 1994 and by the end of the century was in massive use around the world. Today, information is posted on the World Wide Web or is sent via email from one user to another and, depending on speed of service, it is received in seconds or fractions of a second.

The fact that computers connect us person to person through time and space is an extraordinary advance in communication technology. In 1984, there were one thousand home computers, in 1987 ten thousand, in 1989 a hundred thousand, and one million by 1992. The World Wide Web came into existence in 1994. By 1996, we had ten million computers worldwide. The twenty-first century marked the onset of drastic developments in machine learning and the analysis of large volumes of personal user data. The importance of this instantaneous connection between peoples via the internet cannot be overstated.

I vividly remember the 1960s, when Sergio Mondragón and I edited *El Corno Emplumado*. Our goal was to present excellent translations of poetry and prose, making it possible for North American readers to access literature written in Spanish and Latin American readers to access literature written in English. Ours was a worthy effort and is still credited today with building literary bridges. The technology available to us, however, was typical of the times. All communication went through the postal service, and we couldn't afford airmail rates for heavy envelopes containing writing or artwork. We sent everything regular mail, which traveled by ship. Long-distance telephone calls were outside our economic means, and the internet beyond our imagination.

When poets in Buenos Aires or New York or London sent us their work, it took three to four months for it to reach us via a series of national postal services. We would read the submission and send an acceptance or rejection letter, which would take another three to four months to reach the poet in question. Submitting work to an international literary magazine thus took half a year between submission and response. Today, almost all such submissions are done online. The only time lapse is that during which an editor is reading and deciding on whether or not to publish a piece of writing.

Although radio newscasts in the United States began in 1920, and movie newsreels a couple of decades later, mass communication as opposed to the individual message vastly increased with the propaganda produced by both sides during World War II. The Nazis were particularly adept at such messaging. I think of films by Leni Riefenstahl, like *Triumph of the Will* (1935), and the propaganda she created for the Berlin Olympics of 1936. Or Anton Kutter's *Germanics against Pharaonics* (1939), which makes the claim that Germanic tribes predated the knowledge of the ancient Egyptian pharaohs, implying that Aryan artistic genius created the pyramids, an example of using art to falsely validate an absurd and racist theory. Some Nazi Olympic propaganda ended up defying its intent when news reels showed a Black athlete, Jesse Owens, winning several races and the long jump; propaganda produced to exalt the Third Reich instead displayed the tunnel vision of German racism.

In the United States, the Office of War Information directed World War II propaganda. It used posters, radio, newsreels, and feature films, as well as other mediums of communication, to raise approval for the war, get people to support the troops, urge against waste, and entice women into factory jobs vacated by the men who had been called to the front. Patriotism was the central theme. This propaganda employed psychological guilt, fear, name-calling, euphemism, skewed statistics, and convincing testimonials. Our government's most devastating World War II propaganda lie may have been claiming that bombing Hiroshima and Nagasaki was necessary to ending the war, when we now know that the Japanese had already made plans to surrender. Communism would be the United

States' next enemy, and the nation sacrificed hundreds of thousands of Japanese civilians in order to instill fear into the U.S.S.R., a country that had been one of our staunchest wartime allies.

Because posters are often produced quickly to promote urgent ideas, they deserve special attention. Wartime posters generally don't have much artistic merit or staying power; they are vivid and direct and meant to do a job in the moment. Sports posters fall into the same category. But some countries, such as Poland and Cuba, are famous for the significant production of posters that are effective in terms of putting forth an idea and remain highly acclaimed works of art. Technologies such as silkscreen printing became popular precisely because of their use in these posters. This is crossover communication at its most successful.

Since its inception, film has been an important vehicle of mass communication. Although early light techniques such as shadow play and magic lantern preceded the more advanced technologies, the advent of motion pictures is generally dated to the end of the nineteenth century, and the shift from novelty to an established mass entertainment industry came quickly. Production companies and studios were soon established all over the world. Special visual effects followed. Silent films gave way to "talkies," musical scores were commissioned specifically for films and marketed separately as soundtracks, animation and other technologies were developed and quickly improved upon. I can remember the animation artists who drew thousands of separate images to produce figures in movement. Today, this is all done digitally.

Hollywood's golden age is generally considered to have ended in the 1960s, but films continue to have enormous cultural impact. The major Hollywood studios were fiefdoms for many years, establishing social mores for generations. Actresses were either the perfect girl next door or the seductive vamp, the film world's version of virgin or whore. Male leads, even when they might be gay in real life, were projected as the man every woman wants to marry. Gradually, low-budget projects gained attention by showing at arts theaters and festivals. 3D enjoyed a brief popularity, and genres such as musicals and horror films have had their moments of greatest impact.

Subscription platforms such as Netflix, Amazon Prime, and Hulu are now threatening the survival of movie theaters in much the same way that the chain bookstores threatened, and to a large extent wiped out, independent bookstores two decades ago. Pornographic and snuff films have become categories relegated to the shadows but remain a booming business in terms of influence and profit. Home movies gained popularity with the advent of technologies such as 8mm, video, and smartphone cameras. There is no doubt that a variety of film genres retain their ability to move multitudes.

In 1948, right after World War II, television came on the scene. It was developed and spread quickly throughout the 1950s. I grew up in a pre-television era, and radio was my go-to entertainment. After I left home in my late teens, I can remember returning to find my younger sister and brother glued to our family's first black-and-white TV. The creativity encouraged when listening to the radio and having to imagine what each character looked like developed skills that I believe are lacking in generations that receive it all pre-packaged and fed to them on the small screen.

I wonder if television replacing radio as the all-American entertainment mode didn't signal the beginning of everything being classified as entertainment: news reports as well as fictional theater, quiz and game shows, and even commercials. So-called reality shows create impossible standards of behavior; most viewers don't realize that their crisis situations are constructed to woo an audience. Dating shows like *The Bachelor* turn romance into a contest in which contenders are eliminated one by one. Talk show hosts such as Phil Donahue, Larry King, and Oprah Winfrey became household names; Oprah had local-language franchises all over the world and gained a degree of power and influence unusual for a Black woman. Some hosts, such Jerry Springer, capitalized on making guests as uncomfortable as possible; his shows inevitably ended in on-screen brawls that titillated the public's hunger for an all-out fight. Video games, an offshoot of film, offer interactive enticement to youth, and these have become addictive. Some believe they are responsible for the out-of-control violence so prevalent today. (There are several in which the heroes are Nazis or Ku Klux Klan members.) The goal is no longer to inform but to entertain, which often means to lull into acquiescence. And now the prominence of broadcast and cable television is being threatened by online entertainment.

In this complex panorama, intention is important. When is technology used to enhance our lives? When is its goal to inform, to entertain, to manipulate? I think of the Bauhaus, the German art movement launched by Walter Gropius and others in 1919, and influential especially during the 1920s and '30s. It had its own schools in the German cities of Weimar, Dessau, and Berlin, and such artists as Paul Klee, Wassily Kandinsky, and László Moholy-Nagy were central figures. The Bauhaus aimed to marry aesthetics and functionality, giving rise to an industrial design that fashioned chairs that were both elegant and comfortable to sit in, objects of everyday use that not only worked well but were also beautiful. This was a time when we considered progress to be beneficial, something not always easy to do today.

An attitude of intentionality in process is apparent when a mathematician refers to an equation as elegant or beautiful. It is not enough to arrive at the correct answer;

there is the desire to arrive at that answer in as clean, transparent, and aesthetically pleasing a way as possible. Intention affects our lives more dramatically when linked to the withholding or revealing of information accumulated by governments or corporations, the dissemination of which protects those who have access to it and targets those kept in the dark. Many whistleblowers, whose jobs give them access to privileged information, release it because they believe those affected have a right to know. Some are shamed by their prior complicity.

Whistleblowers changed the world in the mid-1990s after a long campaign to demonstrate that cigarettes are injurious to human health. Whistleblowers have also spoken out about the dangers of unproved medications, coal and nuclear power, toxic waste dumps, fracking, and other industrial practices clearly injurious to our health. Over the past decade, whistleblowers in the public perception went from respected citizens to criminals. This shift in popular perception responds to a successful campaign on the part of governments and corporations to discredit and punish them.

Perhaps the most famous example of a U.S. whistleblower who risked his freedom and future to publicize information he believed should be made public is Daniel Ellsberg, an analyst at the RAND Corporation. In 1971, he released thousands of pages of government documents showing how the U.S. government was lying about its involvement in Vietnam. Richard Nixon, a notorious hawk, was president at the time. The *New York Times*, *Washington Post*, and other major newspapers published those documents, and their release helped turn public opinion against the U.S. American war in Southeast Asia. Ellsberg was tried but eventually found innocent. The case went all the way to the Supreme Court, which ruled in favor of free speech.

Today's equivalent of Ellsberg is Edward Snowden. Snowden worked as an analyst for the Central Intelligence

Agency and National Security Agency, among others. The material to which he was privy convinced him that we needed a public discussion about national security and individual privacy. At first, he raised his concerns through internal channels, but they were ignored. By the spring of 2013, while working at the NSA, Snowden had become thoroughly disillusioned. He downloaded thousands of files to his personal hard drive, left his job at a facility in Hawaii, flew to Hong Kong, and handed those files to a group of journalists working for the *Guardian* of London.

The journalists risked their own security by publishing the story—and the documents. Two days later, Snowden tried to fly via Moscow to Ecuador, where he had been promised political asylum by that country's progressive government. The U.S., however, revoked his passport, and the Russians stopped him from traveling on. For a while he was forced to live in the Moscow airport, but Russia finally issued him residency.

Snowden has been transparent about his intentions in releasing classified information. He seeks neither money nor fame but defends his leaks as an effort "to inform the public as to that which is done in their name and that which is done against them." He believes that U.S. citizens have a right to know how much of their privacy is being invaded, and to what ends. In September 2020, a U.S. federal court ruled that the U.S. intelligence's mass surveillance program, which Snowden exposed, was illegal and possibly unconstitutional. Snowden, however, remains a fugitive from justice. He knows that if he were to return to the United States to face a trial, he would most likely be imprisoned. Daniel Ellsberg has publicly advised him to stay away, pointing out that we are living in very different times than the 1970s.

Modern technology has given us extraordinary collective experiences. Gregory and I, and perhaps also his younger sisters Sarah and Ximena, remember the wonder of watching the first human land on the moon in July of 1969. We were in hiding in Mexico at the time, and we viewed the event on a small black-and-white TV at the home of a friend who had taken us in. Billions of people around the world were transfixed by the same image at the very same time. For our family, it was a magical moment in a context of personal confusion and fear. Never before had communication technology brought an event of such magnitude and from the distance of outer space to so many viewers simultaneously.

Each of these inventions has come with its own set of ethical and intellectual issues. They have contracted our sense of space and time, strengthening the conviction some of us have that time is not linear nor space rigidly constructed. Barbara believes that time may be linear on this plane but not necessarily on others. I fluctuate in my sense of what time is and how it behaves, but a purely linear explanation doesn't convince me, especially when I explore my own memory. Consider my having retrieved, a half-century after the fact, the masked memory of my maternal grandparents sexually abusing me; or think about certain other experiences I've had, such as coming to a place I've never visited before and finding it inexplicably familiar.

As someone who came of age during Joseph McCarthy's brutal assault on freedom of expression in the United States, I know how political control of artistic freedom can cast a chill for generations. I was too young to experience the witch hunt personally but had friends who suffered job loss, prison, and, most importantly, a silencing that affected them for the rest of their lives. Some suffered immeasurably greater loss; Julius and Ethel Rosenberg were falsely convicted of being atomic spies. They were executed, leaving their two small sons without their parents. As a poet, I matured in an atmosphere in which one knew one could write about some things but not others. I had to go to live in Mexico in order to come in contact with poets who wrote about everything: love, fear, death, the land, and, yes, also the social and political issues that concerned them. I believe that move saved me from a kind of self-censorship that plagues many of my contemporaries.

Our notions of what memory itself is are also challenged. Our ideas about privacy as well. Clearly, every passing day brings more access to information. But what sort of information? The internet is flooded with disinformation and misinformation, much of it purposefully disseminated to feed political, ideological, or marketing interests. And the data about each of us that is currently being collected and analyzed by governments and corporations is vaster and more detailed than most of us can imagine. These databanks don't only register our physical characteristics: age, race or ethnicity, gender, national origin, and sexual orientation; they keep track of our movements, health, education, tastes, and, most threateningly, our vulnerabilities and fears. This information is used to create fabricated needs in large numbers of people, push us to do things we may not want to do, doubt reasonable assumptions, or think thoughts that wouldn't otherwise occur to us. It can also be used to control the deepest recesses of our emotional lives. In fact, it is doing all this today, although we don't yet know to what degree.

Communication surrounds and engulfs us even as we ourselves invent new technologies with which we can broaden its reach and new modalities of expression that enrich it. In important ways, I believe that art is an antidote to this onslaught. In this regard, the idea of "art and technology" might better be expressed as "art feeding and challenging technology" or "technology enriching and subverting art." It has often been said that art is a different kind of truth. Or that fiction tells the truth that history cannot. Never are these statements more relevant than when our perception of reality is twisted by political screed. Each culture, each age, contributes to increasing art's variety and richness. I came of age as "happenings" emerged on the New York art scene; the public was invited to participate in interactive theatrical events. Over the past couple of decades in the United States alone, hip hop and slam poetry have become enormously popular. New forms and artistic genres emerge constantly, reflecting changing cultural norms.

This too can be both positive and negative. Take, for example, Donald Trump's war against truth in political discourse. It was not a new phenomenon for politicians to lie, on the left as well as on the right. But by calling accurate reporting "fake news," journalists "the enemies of the people," and repeating his politically motivated lies over and over again, Trump succeeded in convincing at least seventy million U.S. Americans that they must not trust what they hear and read from respected information sources. This massive assault on truth in language created a reliable underpinning for Trump's crimes. He didn't have to commit the crimes and then lie to cover them up. The lies were already firmly in place, providing him with a movement of neo-fascist shock troops who march to the tune of a man who is as delusional as he is criminal.

New technologies are developed all the time to deliver political propaganda in convincing ways. One that isn't all that sophisticated but has been enormously effective in the United States in recent years is the transmission of robocalls, automated political, marketing or even service messages that say anything from "If you can't get to the polls today, don't worry; you can always go tomorrow" to "Your Social Security account has been hacked; please press one to learn more." Hundreds of thousands of these can be generated automatically. They are aimed at getting the recipient to do something—or refrain from doing something—that benefits the robocaller. You don't even need to fall for the scam. Simply answering the phone puts you on a list of "good targets" who may be vulnerable to further attempts. Robocalls are an example of technology serving the lie.

Statistics are frequently manipulated to "prove" skewed situations or opinions. When we are told, for example, that more people voted in the recent U.S. presidential election than ever before in our history, we are not told that our nation's population has also grown exponentially. It is true that a record number of voters went to the polls, but it is also useful to understand the context. Many studies are published without naming the sponsoring institution; should we trust a pharmaceutical company to assess the success or failure of a drug that it has developed? I always remember my friend, feminist biologist Ruth Hubbard, explaining that claiming one out of nine women will get breast cancer is a distortion designed to convince us we must submit to regular mammograms. Why not say eight out of nine women will not get breast cancer? Note that I am not advocating against mammograms but simply stating the biased ways such statistics are put forth. These are but a few examples of how statistical analysis can be presented differently to encourage different outcomes and mindsets. Polls are similarly manipulated to favor a particular position or to convince those following them that support is growing or diminishing for a candidate or idea in which they have an interest. Too often the desired answer is implicit in the way the question is asked.

We also see a tendency, with the subsequent popularity of new technological modalities, in which the development of each platform seems to reduce an individual's need to express themselves creatively. A collective intellectual laziness is inevitably the result. When we wrote letters by hand, penmanship (a design skill) was required along with the expression of our own ideas in our own way. The Palmer Method was all the rage when I was learning to write.

Typewriters eliminated the need for penmanship; schools in the United States stopped teaching cursive writing and concentrated on teaching students to print each letter separately. With computers, we no longer had the need for changing the machine's ink-soaked ribbon, dealing with messy carbon paper, fading second sheets, or white-out. "Cut and paste" as well as online dictionaries and thesauruses are at our fingertips.

Emails still demand that we express ourselves, although Google now offers us readymade phrases such as "thank you," "will do," or "I agree" that relieve us of the responsibility for creating such responses ourselves. Emoticons are also available; a smiling or frowning face, a bright heart or thumbs-up conveys an emotion so we don't have to express it in our own words. These might be considered modern-day glyphs used to communicate ideas and meaning, but as such they are a poor lexicon. Saving time is emphasized in modern-day living, but when we concentrate on saving time, we inevitably lose skills that enrich our creativity.

From email, younger people have moved rapidly to WhatsApp, a platform that favors brief messages, Twitter that limits each tweet to 280 characters, and Instagram where people post a single image, often without any caption at all. This progression, that so obviously trends toward using fewer and fewer of our own original ideas and words, threatens our collective capacity for self-expression.

Because of the great number of right-wing messages that flood social media and even our own inboxes, a mistrust of science and a wholesale swallowing of conspiracy theories plague the United States today. Class divisions are no longer only economic in nature but increasingly informed by access to reliable information. The divide between that part of the world population that can use the internet and that part of it that cannot is also made much greater because of this. In countries like the U.S., perhaps 90% of the population has routine access to online information. In some parts of Africa, it may be as low as 5%. It is clear that a whole new reality is being constructed for those with access to digital communication by virtue of their ability to access whatever currently dominates informational space. This further separates the haves from the have-nots. The vast numbers of those around the world who do not have access to the internet are living in another century. It's always about balance, and it's not easy to know where to draw the lines.

All of this also leads to a pervasive mistrust of our own experience. We have the common example of people going to their cell phone or computer to get a reading on the weather rather than opening the window and looking outside. It's great to have those online weather services in order to be able to find out what the weather is doing somewhere else, but when we replace our own ability to open a window with such a technological solution, we are losing real contact with our environment. Similarly, too many people with health problems of one sort or another favor information put out by companies that make medications for those problems rather than searching for an independent study, learning to trust a health professional who comes from a more educated perspective, or listening to what their own bodies are telling them.

There is also the interesting, often alarming, issue of what we might call "public intimacy." This is the prevalence of people today sharing extremely personal information via social media with the entire world. For example, one "friends" others on Facebook, few of whom are friends in any real sense of that designation. Many users of public platforms post their most intimate thoughts and even photographs they may later wish they had never made public. Once online, it is difficult if not impossible to delete such posts. Many a job applicant has failed to win a position because those researching their online profile have discovered posts or images incompatible with the company's ethics or preferences. Even more tragic are the suicides, many among adolescents, caused by online bullying. It would be wonderful if we could address the social causes of loneliness and isolation rather than simply discuss their digital footprint.

It is clear that social media has great benefits as well as disturbing problems. The powerful political movements that led to the so-called Arab Spring depended heavily on social media to direct people to meeting places as well as to proselytize positions. Social media has been used in this way throughout the world. In the United States, Occupy, Black Lives Matter, and #MeToo have reached millions through Facebook and Twitter. So did Donald Trump with his repetition of lies and baseless accusations. I think history shows that old-fashioned person-to-person organizing makes for deeper and longer-lasting commitment. There are obvious contradictions between mass propaganda and a profundity of analysis.

As I write, the COVID-19 pandemic has pushed poets like myself to virtual platforms such as Zoom for performances, interviews, and panels. Since March 2020, I have been doing at least four of these a week, sometimes more. I have done them in English and Spanish, participated in poetry festivals and public forums, launched new books, and supported the work of others. In Mexico, one of my events got more than seven thousand views. Often a panel or discussion or reading will draw only thirty or forty people to the event itself, but then a video posted on Facebook or YouTube will continue to receive visits into the hundreds.

These virtual events have allowed me to reach people in Mexico, Colombia, Chile, Uruguay, Argentina, Italy, Germany, Cuba, Ecuador, Nicaragua, Ireland, England, Canada, and Australia, and throughout the United States. Had I done them live, I would have had to travel around the world and probably wouldn't have had more than a couple of hundred people at each event, if that many. So, these platforms have enabled me to reach out in ways I never could before. And they have brought other benefits as well. For example, in a small class I taught online, the students all communicated from their homes. I had a glimpse of how each of them lives. Some were participating in front of unmade beds, others in studios where I could see some of the art on their walls or books on their shelves. There is personal connection at these virtual events that often surprises me. An intimacy that is both false and real, of course, but nevertheless sparks my interest.

After observing Gregory's class, watching Martin's presentation, listening to others in the course ask questions and make comments, and viewing those two episodes of *Nova* with Barbara and sharing our ideas, I am mostly left with a profound amazement at how different cultures have developed writing systems, the similarity of some of these systems in places distant from one another, the interweaving of art and technology, and the ethical questions raised by the internet and World Wide Web. Perhaps for a poet like myself, the most exciting areas left to be explored are those of language and language culture. The technological advances, like so many things, are neither all good nor all bad. Yet we must be vigilant. It is probably too late for that vigilance to mean anything, though. The technologies have largely moved beyond ethics.

Abandoning Either/Or

IN TWO ESSAYS IN THIS COLLECTION, one about the removal of racist monuments and statues, the other about the #MeToo movement and how important it has been for women but how it has occasionally gone too far and irrevocably damaged men whose misconduct was either very far in the past or didn't rise to the level of sexual assault, I have tried something that is difficult to do. I wanted to show my total support for an important movement while at the same time expressing concerns about some aspects of it. I do not want to come off as uncertain. I confidently proclaim my loyalties. Neither do I want to assume some liberal and cowardly "devil's advocate" role; there are few positions I respect less. I would like to put forth my radical advocacy while at the same time asking for a degree of nuance that allows us to avoid fanaticism.

This nuanced position is not an easy one from which to write. It leaves one open to rebukes from the left as well as to vilification from the right. Needless to say, I expect the latter. The former is disappointing, and I have experienced it often: for example, when I pointed out the Cuban Revolution's early anti-feminist stance, its periodic upsurge in censorship or discrimination against homosexuals; when I pleaded with the U.S. left to consider gender inequality along with class contradiction; and when I publicly stated that Daniel Ortega's longtime sexual abuse of his stepdaughter renders him unfit to be president of Nicaragua. Whenever I've made these criticisms of a revolutionary movement that I otherwise support, some on the left have accused me of "washing dirty laundry in public" and have argued that such criticism only provides arguments to the enemy.

So, not an easy position from which to write; but, I would argue, a necessary one. If we want social change to succeed, we must be willing to speak up when the familiar cry of "unity at all costs" is used to conceal errors, silence criticism, or avoid discussion of issues that invariably have long-range effects on a society's values and its ability to include every group in its project of change.

Why is the left so often reluctant to look at these issues in a complex way?

It may be that some traditional Marxists are stuck in the belief that class is society's fundamental contradiction and that new relations of production will automatically bring about desired social and cultural change. But so much has been written in recent years that dispels this narrowness of vision that it is hard to accept that it persists in people who are truly trying to create a more egalitarian society. Not to mention the fact that we now have ample evidence that only by understanding the interrelated problems of all social groups can we solve our problems in a way that leaves no one out.

It may be because, at a particular moment, a revolution is under a great deal of pressure from outside forces trying to destroy it and internal forces jockeying for power. But if this were true, when that pressure subsides, the revolutionary leadership should welcome constructive criticism. History has shown us this hasn't been the case.

It may be because the leadership is imprisoned in old either/or ways of thinking and incapable of understanding the importance of in-depth analysis. But if this is true, those in power should be able to address more complex issues as education becomes more accessible. In Cuba, where more than sixty years have gone by since its revolutionary victory in 1959, the population as a whole has one of the highest educational levels of any nation on earth. Yet most of these issues remain unaddressed—at least in forums in which the general public has a real voice. On the other hand, we often judge past errors without situating them in the historic period in which they occurred. For example, in the 1960s when the Cuban Revolution considered homosexuals to be social degenerates, this was the way most societies saw sexual difference. As a society matures, one can expect correction of outdated attitudes and discriminatory practices. Cuba has moved with the times on this issue, but, sadly, many countries have not.

Or it may simply be that a mostly male, mostly light-skinned, still-historic leadership doesn't really want to relinquish its privilege. Patriarchy is impressive in its ability to embed itself in every social, political, economic, and cultural arena. Addressing gender, race, sexual identity, freedom of expression, and dissent threatens a privileged class that has always profited by avoiding in-depth discussion of such issues.

Which is not to say that in Cuba change hasn't happened. It has. Early rejection of feminism has softened with the years, although the party in power has yet to make a gender analysis of society. The party stopped outright discrimination against and abuse of homosexuals, and the situation for those of non-heteronormative sexual and gender identities has improved. The population has become more conscious of endemic racism, mostly because Cubans of color have demanded this. In the early 1990s, censorship was called out in the arts, and differences of expression began to be respected.

But when the Cuban Revolution has had the will to effect a monumental change in a short period of time, it has done so brilliantly. One example is the 1961 literacy campaign in which secondary school students skipped class for a year and taught an entire nation to read and write. Another is the way in which universal healthcare has been shaped to meet the needs of the Cuban people. The Revolution has been capable of extraordinary feats. Yet women continue to face obstacles that should have been dealt with long ago, dark-skinned Cubans remain underrepresented in leadership positions, and marriage equality is still not the law of the land on the Caribbean island.

When you love something, you want it to be as good as it can be. I love the Cuban Revolution, and I express criticism because I believe it can be better.

But let's look at our own country, one that continues to call itself a democracy although it strayed so far from that aspiration under the Trump administration. Between 2016 and 2020, our population became dramatically polarized; perhaps not since our Civil War has it been so divided. Roughly half our citizenry engaged in fanatical all-out loyalty to Trump and what he stands for; in spite of each and every egregious or criminal act, it continues to support him without question. The other half saw his narcissism, racism, misogyny, xenophobia, lying, disregard for the earth, and repudiation of science for what they are: frighteningly dangerous and a prelude to fascism. Because the stakes were

Abandoning Either/Or

so high for everyone, most members of both groups simply screamed our reasoning at the top of our lungs, unable or unwilling to shape our language in ways that might be understood by our opponents. We did not speak with one another but at one another.

In many academic circles, thinking for its own sake—the beauty and freedom to contemplate ideas and see where they lead—has been vitiated by political considerations. Intellectualism and politics have somehow become oppositional. Thinking for thinking's sake is no longer considered useful.

Was there room for nuance? Would nuance even have been possible in that political climate? We may answer these questions differently depending on whether we are talking about a discussion within a family, an organization, a community, or among the broader public. The answers may also vary depending on the moment; for example, in the midst of the death-dealing forest fires recently engulfing the western part of the United States, some who previously accepted Trump's claim that global warming had nothing to do with them were willing to listen to the scientific arguments dispelling that irresponsible claim. By the same token, the coronavirus pandemic sickened and killed without regard to political positions, and many who have lost loved ones now concede that the safety precautions spurned by Trump might have saved their lives.

By looking at the different sides of an important issue, I am saying let's talk about these things and with this nuance before it's too late. Before valuable years of social change are lost to either/or politics. Before homosexuals are confined to labor camps as in the early days of the Cuban Revolution or tens of thousands of refugee families are torn apart by today's U.S. immigration policy.

Truth is not to be feared, no matter how complex its presentation. And it almost always needs complexity to be truth. As poet and philosopher Adrienne Rich wrote: "Lying is done with words and also with silence."[1] Failure to address the difficult aspects of important issues is tantamount to lying.

---

1. In the title essay of *Lies, Secrets, and Silence.* W. W. Norton, 1979.

Acknowledgments

SOME OF THESE ESSAYS were published, often in a different form, on The Black Earth Institute's blog and in *The Blue Nib* in Dublin, Ireland; *Revista Abril* in Miami, Florida; and *Dooney's Cafe* in Vancouver, BC. Excerpts from previous books are credited within the essays themselves. A Spanish-language edition will also be published in 2021 by Heredad in Mexico City.

I also want to acknowledge Zach Hively's expert and thoughtful editing, which helped shape the book you hold in your hands. Great editors are rare, and I am grateful to have had his wisdom.

About the author

MARGARET RANDALL is a feminist poet, essayist, oral historian, translator, teacher, and photographer with a long history of social activism in Mexico, Cuba, Nicaragua, and the United States. She is the author, translator, and editor of nearly two hundred books and cofounder of *El Corno Emplumado / The Plumed Horn*, a bilingual journal that published more than seven hundred writers from thirty-five countries. She fought deportation by the U.S. government, which claimed her writing subversive, and won her case. She has been recently awarded the Poet of Two Hemispheres Prize, the Haydée Santamaría medal, an honorary doctorate of letters from the University of New Mexico, the Democratic Project Paulo Freire Award, and the George Garrett Award.

She lives in Albuquerque, New Mexico, with her wife, the artist Barbara Byers.

Casa Urraca Press

WE ARE A HOME for words that speak to the soul and stimulate thought. We publish daring, eloquent authors of poetry and creative nonfiction. And we offer workshops with our authors and other artists.

Every writer and every publisher has a slant. Ours tilts toward the richness of the high desert, where all are welcome who manage to find their way.

We are proudly centered somewhere near Abiquiu, New Mexico. Visit us at casaurracaltd.com for exquisite editions of our books and for workshop registration.

www.ingramcontent.com/pod-product-compliance
Lightning Source LLC
Chambersburg PA
CBHW031102080526
44587CB00011B/790